Fort Canning Hill:
Exploring Singapore's Heritage and Nature

By Melissa Diagana and Jyoti Angresh

ORO
EDITIONS

FOREWORD

I congratulate Jyoti Angresh and Melissa Diagana for writing this important book. I thank ORO editions and NHB's Heritage Industry Incentive Programme (or HI²P) for supporting heritage enthusiasts such as Jyoti and Melissa in the documentation and promotion of Singapore's heritage.

Fort Canning has a special place in the history of Singapore and in the hearts of history-loving Singaporeans. Let me elaborate.

First, Fort Canning possesses the evidence to support the view of Kwa Chong Guan, Derek Heng and Tan Tai Yong, the authors of "Singapore: A 700 Year History", that Singapore's history did not begin in 1819. They argue in their book that Singapore has been settled since the 14th century. During excavations in 1926, for the construction of a reservoir, near the Keramat Iskandar Shah, the workers found a large cache of gold ornaments. One of the objects, an armlet, has the face of Kala, the Indian deity, engraved on it. Experts have identified it as reminiscent of the craftsmanship of the Majapahit period in the 14th Century. The armlet is on display at the National Museum of Singapore.

According to Sejarah Melayu, the founder of Singapore, Seri Teri Buana, aka Sang Nila Utama, built his palace on top of Fort Canning, then known as Bukit Larangan (Forbidden Hill). Being aware of the historical significance of this legend, Raffles also built his residence on top of the hill, which was re-named the Singapore Hill. It was subsequently re-named as the Government Hill and finally, as Fort Canning Hill, in honour of Viscount Charles John Canning, the first Viceroy of India, who had never visited Singapore.

Second, Fort Canning has an interesting military history. The British had built a fort on the hill, in order to defend Singapore from possible attacks from the sea. During the Second World War, the British General defending Singapore, Arthur E Percival, had his headquarters on Fort Canning.

It was here, in his bunkers, that General Percival decided to surrender to the Japanese. On the evening of 15 February 1942, General Percival surrendered to Lt-General Yamashita at the Ford Factory on Bukit Timah Road. The factory now houses a reflective gallery on the war and the Japanese Occupation, under the management of the National Archives of Singapore.

Third, Fort Canning is the home of many other stories. It has one of the oldest cemeteries in Singapore. Many famous people were buried there and they include George Drumgoole Coleman who designed and constructed many of Singapore's colonial-era public buildings and roads; Sir Jose D'Almeida Carvalho, the Portuguese Consul-General; Charles Spottiswoode; and the Armenian merchant Aristakes Sarkies. In fact, the Melaka "wife" of William Farquhar, Antoinette Clement, was also interred there. Although Farquhar subsequently married a Scottish woman, the descendants of Farquhar's Melaka wife have been more successful than those of his Scottish wife. One of the descendants is Margaret Trudeau who was once married to the charismatic Prime Minister of Canada, Pierre Trudeau. When the cemetery was converted into a park, a number of tombstones and statues from the cemetery were transferred and placed within the garden compound of the nearby Armenian Church of St Gregory the Illuminator. Another cemetery on Fort Canning is the Keramat Iskandar Shah, reputed to be the resting place of Sultan Iskandar Shah. There is no documentary proof of this assertion, but people continue to make offerings to the soul of whoever is buried there.

Fort Canning is a place of history, nature, mystery and romance. Today, it is used to stage concerts. It is also the home of a heritage hotel, the Singapore Dance Theatre, and a Second World War bunker. I hope that the thousands of people who flock there will enjoy reading this book. It will enrich their experience of being on hallowed ground.

Professor Tommy Koh

Honorary Chairman
National Heritage Board

THOUGHTS ON THE BOOK

No landmark in Singapore can compare with Fort Canning Hill. The site encompasses seven centuries of history. Scholars are just beginning to understand the rich tapestry of culture which the first inhabitants of Singapore, who came from all over Asia, wove as they built dwellings on terraces cut into the hill's slopes.

Despite the intense activity of the 19th and 20th centuries, Fort Canning Hill preserves an amazing quantity of tangible relics of the past. I have spent many hours working at archaeological sites on the hill, and despite the park's location at the very centre of downtown Singapore, it is still possible to imagine how the place must have appeared in the 14th century.

In the early 19th century, the British considered the hill to be the crowning glory of their new settlement. It is probable that the ancient Malays who ruled this island felt just as much respect for the hill. It is one of three important hills in Malay history. The first was Seguntang Hill in Sumatra, where the first Malay ruler Sang Nila Utama first appeared before migrating to Singapore (then called Temasek). When he died, according to Malay tradition, he was buried on this hill of Singapore. The third one is now called St. Paul's Hill in Melaka. All three of the ancient capitals of the Malays had exactly the same layout: a palace on a hill overlooking an estuary which served as a great harbour and thoroughfare for local commerce.

Early Chinese visitors referred to it as "the hill of Temasek", or as Pancur ("spring of water"; several other Malay capitals in Johor and Sumatra had the same name). The ancient inhabitants no doubt viewed the hill with more than a tinge of awe; for them it represented Mount Meru, the mountain at the centre of the universe, where Indra, king of the gods, presided; it would have reminded Buddhists of the sermons which Gautama himself preached on peaks such as the Mount of Eagles in India.

Fort Canning Hill is one of Singapore's greatest treasures. The country is extremely fortunate to have such a gem of history and nature so easily accessible and so well preserved. May it ever remain so! I hope that by presenting the significance of the historical and natural resources on the hill, this book will enable visitors to understand the significance of their surroundings so as to enjoy this place to the utmost of its potential.

Associate Professor John Miksic

National University of Singapore
Head, Archaeological Unit at Institute
of Southeast Asian Studies

Located in the heart of Singapore's city centre, Fort Canning Hill is built on a hill that has a history of 700 years. Over the centuries, the hill has gone through many transformations, from being the home of ancient Malay kings and the colonial government, to a military base during the Second World War, and its current incarnation as a public park for recreation.

Fort Canning Hill has a special place in our national heritage, and in our people's memories. Hundreds visit the park every month – whether to have picnics, attend concerts, or watch performances. The park also draws scores of wedding couples because its lush greenery, expansive grounds and graceful colonial buildings provide attractive backdrops for photographs.

Yet not many know that Fort Canning Hill was where Singapore's first botanical garden was located. Today, a wide variety of flora and fauna still flourishes within its grounds. Fort Canning Hill is a reflection of Singapore's commitment to balance urbanisation and biodiversity conservation. It plays an important role in Singapore's vision to be a City in a Garden, a bustling city characterised by pervasive greenery, thriving biodiversity and a passionate community.

I am pleased that the National Parks Board is part of this project, as it will provide Singaporeans and visitors insights into one of this country's most culturally - and historically - important landmarks.

With this book, I hope that Singaporeans will have a deeper appreciation for Fort Canning Hill, its role in Singapore's ever-changing landscape, as well as its contribution to the transformation of Singapore into a City in a Garden.

Poon Hong Yuen

Chief Executive Officer
National Parks Board

While everyone in Singapore may know where Fort Canning Hill is, and perhaps even visited it a few times, I can't imagine that many know the details of its history, the diversity of its flora and fauna, or its importance in the story of Singapore over the centuries.

Melissa Diagana and Jyoti Angresh, in their beautiful and comprehensive new book on this landmark hill, aim to change this. In these pages, they recount the various names and incarnations of the hill that has been home to a palace, a lighthouse, bathing princesses, cemeteries and a community swimming pool, just to name a few. The authors also share some of the legends surrounding this ancient mound.

Natural history gets it due as well with the many plants and animals that have made Fort Canning their home getting fascinating coverage. From this book, I learned about the "plant-insect mutualism" between figs and fig wasps, and even recipes are included for dishes that can be made from ingredients found at the park. Also, I finally now know why that large bronze nutmeg is sitting in front of ION Orchard!

While an outdoor concert at Fort Canning is certainly a fun way to spend an evening, a visit to Fort Canning Hill in daylight, armed with the knowledge and insights gleaned from this book, promises to be an engaging and thoroughly pleasurable experience and one not to be missed by anyone interested in Singapore's past.

Brett Alison Gold

Managing Editor
Living in Singapore (12th edition)

Nature and man together in the park, designed by Eng Siak Loy, carved by Villa Frangipani.

In the heart of Singapore lies this multifaceted hill waiting to be explored.

A walk around Fort Canning Hill can become anything a visitor wants it to be:

• A biology class

• A physical fitness session

• A history lesson

• An art appreciation outing

• A family picnic

• A bird-watching gathering

• A relaxing stroll

The park exemplifies the melding of nature and history and showcases preservation and development in this island nation perfectly.

Fort Canning Hill encourages visitors to appreciate the rich and varied heritage of Singapore, its appeal transcending its immediate environment.

The hill has much in common with other parks around the globe: A green park, that has evolved from an experiment in economic botany; ancient ruins encouraging one to muse upon the past, present, and future; a vibrant space for cultural explorations; and hilltop views of the old and the new that together constitute a dynamic city.

It is a hidden jewel waiting to be discovered . . .

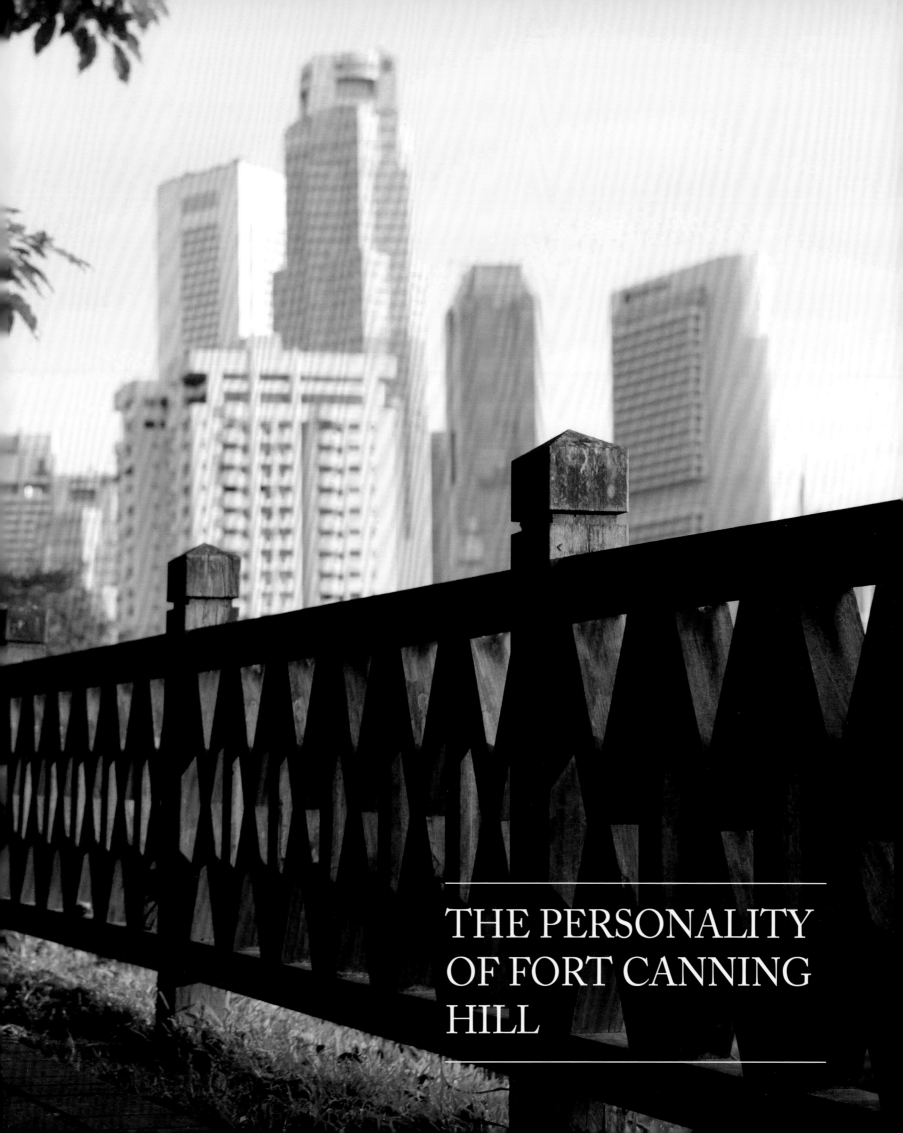

THE PERSONALITY OF FORT CANNING HILL

A Hill, First and Foremost

The early morning sunlight filters down through the canopy of leaves. A break in the leaf cover allows a ray of sun to reach the path, where a Changeable lizard basks before starting its day. An Asian koel perched on a nearby branch peers out with its disconcertingly bright red eyes and makes its haunting calls. Another day is beginning at Fort Canning Hill.

In a relatively flat country that is a small dot on the world map, Fort Canning Hill is a charming elevated oasis, nestled within a frenetic urban environment.

First and foremost, the physical geography of Fort Canning Hill has defined its personality over the centuries. In humid Singapore, an elevated hill with its cooling breezes is a prize, and it is not hard to see why Prince Sang Nila Utama chose it as the location for his palace when he first landed here from Sumatra at the turn of the 14th century.

Seven hundred years ago, none of Singapore's other hills were as strategically located as Fort Canning Hill, which was next to the bustling community around the Singapore River. Furthermore, the hill's summit provided a view of the river mouth, and a freshwater spring along its slopes provided drinking water for the palace.

All of these characteristics – climate, view, river, spring – led Sir Stamford Raffles to choose the same hill 500 years later to build his bungalow. While the attractive elements of the hill have remained constant over the centuries, the feeling the hill imparts to visitors and residents has certainly evolved. Although there was a military presence on the hill until the 1970s, by the early 20th century, there was no longer a need for defence, nor for port surveillance. Trees were planted on a large scale to transform the denuded hill into a recreational haven.

Nearly 200 years after Raffles' landing, the breezes and the view are still drawing visitors to the park on Fort Canning Hill. Today, the connection the hill makes with people evokes a sense of romance, some nostalgia, mystery and perhaps peace.

1 Good morning, Fort Canning Hill!

2 A koel calling from the trees.

3 View seaward from the 14th century palace, as depicted in the online video game "World of Temasek".

4 A similar view, five centuries later (*View of Singapore from Government Hill, 1837* by artist W.C. Smith and engraver C.J. Hullmandel).

opposite A hill first and foremost.

> The island of Singapore consists of a multitude of small hills, three or four hundred feet high, the summit of many of which are still covered with virgin forest.

— A.R. Wallace, 1854/1862, The Malay Archipelago

A Botanic Garden

Although civilisations throughout recorded history have maintained various types of botanical gardens, early modern European botanical gardens began to be established by the mid-16th century. At first, their primary mission was to grow medicinal plants, and to educate doctors and apothecaries. They quickly evolved into gardens showcasing exotic plants and plants of economic importance.

When Raffles arrived in "Singapura" in 1819, he had hoped to develop economically valuable crops that could be grown in tropical climates. Within a year of his arrival, precious nutmeg and clove trees were planted on the north slope of Fort Canning Hill. A few years later, Raffles' personal interest in botany led to this garden being expanded into the "Botanic & Experimental Garden", devoted to tropical spices and produce.

The historical gardens at Fort Canning Hill were to become instrumental in the dialogue between nature and culture in Singapore.

An Urban Park

In many urban landscapes, Man and nature are intimately entwined, and Fort Canning is no exception.

The hill that Sang Nila Utama found was covered in tropical hardwood jungle. He and subsequent kings cleared enough land for the palace and gardens of fruit trees. After their departure at the end of the 14th century, the hill was rapidly overgrown. The thick overgrowth and the fact that local myth of it being haunted discouraged ordinary folk from climbing up the hill made it a safe haven for robbers and others living on the outskirts of society.

When Raffles landed in Singapore in the early 19th century, lowland evergreen forest covered nearly the entire island, Fort Canning Hill included. The British industriously went about scalping the hill, and gone were any trees obstructing views of the hilltop and the bustling harbour. Already in 1833, a Mr. Aliquis complained in a letter to the editor of the *Singapore Chronicle and Commercial Register*, that a "beautiful grove of trees which grew on the Government Hill (unrivalled by any such in all these Straits). . . has been cut down" so that (an obviously important yet unnamed) someone could see the flagstaff from his office.

But by 1859, everyone had become used to the lack of trees, leading one journalist to write glowingly in *The Straits Times* of the pleasant evening strolls one could take up the hill, unencumbered by trees or houses.

1 A torch ginger flower.

2 Nutmeg and mace.

3 1837 view of the denuded hill, by Barthélemy Lauvergne.

4 An urban park.

Over the next century, most people in town were too busy doing things to realise that it would be nice to stop and smell the roses. Though now many of us living in large cities take for granted the presence of a green swath in our midst, in Singapore before World War II, there were not many parks other than the Botanic Gardens.

Finally, though, the light was seen, and just before the outbreak of the war, a major tree-planting effort began for the future King George V Park, which would eventually occupy the southwestern section of today's Fort Canning Hill. At the time, what is now Clemenceau Avenue was an eyesore of abandoned railroad yards, and the entire area was so ugly and poor that one citizen wrote to *The Straits Times* wondering why the city should even bother to beautify a part of town not frequented by "Beautiful People". King George V Park would become a welcome haven for many, including the inhabitants of the neighbouring shophouse slums, where children played and adults relaxed.

opposite page Grassy slopes on the park.

above A 1985 view of Fort Canning Hill, when it was then called Central Park.

A more enlightened writer of a 1950 article in *The Straits Times* praised the park and dared to dream bigger: "A bolder dream, and that is the conversion of the whole of Fort Canning Hill into a public park – a veritable green island in the heart of the city. . . Fort Canning Hill can be converted into one of the most unusual and most beautiful city parks in the world." His sentiments were shared by many. King George V Jubilee Park was expanded and rechristened Central Park in the 1970s. It was enlarged once again and renamed Fort Canning Hill, when then Prime Minister Lee Kuan Yew planted an inaugural fruit tree in 1981.

This small city-state has an evolving relationship with its increasingly urban environment. In the case of this park, Singapore has – deliberately or not – been applying the tenets of landscape urbanism, by allowing the landscape to organise the city around it, and thus enhance the urban experience.

A Microcosm of Singapore

Fort Canning is literally a microcosm of Singapore, being witness to and reflecting almost 700 years of Singapore's history.

The park in its current state is the result of an organic growth that has slowly evolved over time. The fact that it is a little hill at the edge of a river has been the reason it attracted much attention over the centuries. Collecting many interesting secrets and taking on so many colours, it has developed a multifaceted personality that reflects both the past and the present.

From the heyday of the Malay kings of "Temasek" town until Raffles' arrival, the hill was known as "Bukit Larangan", or the Forbidden Hill. Sultan Iskandar Shah had supposedly forbidden commoners to visit the hill so as to prevent them from spying on his wives and concubines bathing in the spring. Reflecting the culture of the times, this injunction stayed in the collective memory of the settlement, and long after there was no longer a palace there, people continued to avoid the hill. Some believe the sultan to be buried on its slopes, which likely gave rise to the legend that it was haunted. So fearful was the populace of the ghosts that the British could not rely on local manpower to clear the its jungle-covered slopes, and had to recruit Malays from Melaka.

1 A view of Marina Bay Sands Hotel taken from the site of Raffles' original house.

2 The *keramat*, or Muslim shrine, dedicated to Sultan Iskandar Shah, by artist Kit Madula.

3 The *orang laut* (sea gypsies) living along the coast, designed by Eng Siak Loy, carved by Villa Frangipani.

The ghosts of the 20th century:

During World War II, the Malayan Command barracks on the hill were occupied by the Japanese army. They did not stay long, though, as they were awakened by disturbances during the night – which the local Malays attributed to the occupant of the ancient tomb!

Between the 17th and early 19th centuries, first the Portuguese and then the Dutch colonial powers controlled most of the ports and trade in the Southeast Asian region. Singapore was sparsely populated during this time with approximately 1,000 indigenous people, including the Malays who lived in *kampongs* (villages) and the *orang laut* (sea gypsies), who lived around the Singapore River (at the base of Fort Canning Hill), the Kallang River, Telok Blangah and along the Johor Straits.

When the British first arrived, Fort Canning charmed them with its strategic location overlooking the harbour, pleasantly cooler air and a history to boot. By the time the hill changed names from "Forbidden Hill" to "Government Hill" or "Singapore Hill" in mid-19th century, it housed residences of colonial leaders from Raffles' first bungalow to the subsequent Governor's residence.

A flagstaff, along with a lighthouse and a time-ball were established to serve society and to aid port trade. The flying of a flag at daylight, the firing of a gun at night, and the dropping of the time-ball helped to mark time as well as keep the community linked and updated.

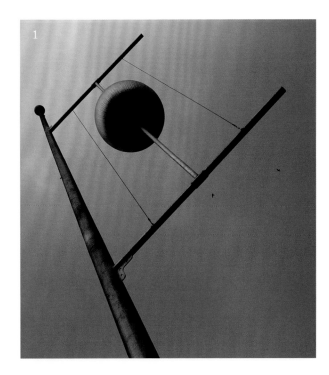

All this time, the hill was reflecting and changing the daily life of people who lived around it. The cultural imprint of the British on Fort Canning is seen to this day in the architecture of numerous buildings still standing.

The civil use of Fort Canning Hill gave way to military use when the Government House was demolished by the British to build a fort around 1860 on the top of the hill. This was to be used in the case of any rebellion or threat of war, especially threat from the sea.

This fort was named after Viscount Charles John Canning, the last Governor-General of India under the British East India Company, and the first Viceroy of India under Crown rule. The hill has since then been known as "Fort Canning Hill".

Fort Canning Hill has undergone several changes over time. Its top was levelled off for a fort, and then gutted for the creation of the reservoir. Its original trees were removed, and 150 years later, other trees - several foreign to Southeast Asia - were planted. Its Botanic & Experimental Garden was developed during the first half of the 19th century, and today there remains a token Spice Garden for educational purposes. It reflects a blend of Asian and Western cultural influences and is a true reflection of Singapore itself. The park is constantly adapting itself to the society around it.

1 Timeball.

2 Singapore's society on Government Hill, reflected in this 1846 painting by John Turnbull Thomson.

3 Singapore's society on Fort Canning Hill in 2009.

4 Lord Canning.

A Forest in Poetry

The first sounds of the tabla
like a god's knuckle gently

knocking against the heart's
resounding door, then your

voice, followed by the others,
rivalling, as if at war,

but I prefer to envision trees
plunging skywards into

light, oblivious of each other
yet fuelled by that sustained

impulse to swell, to ornament
a single chant into endless

branches of pure yearning,
eventuate in a vertiginous

forest of sound, each high note
sewn into a chord vast and

dense as the canopy of trees,
then a peace as when the wind

pauses in its marathon across
the landscape to catch its

breath, then begins again to
go; trees shrug off their awe,

revving up, flexing every leaf,
twig and branch, set once more

to sway, the same way your
phrase — the final solo now —

spirals up like a gold vine to
recapture height, or how those

of us willing to lose our hours
to your melody commence

once more to move our heads,
shaping a new infinity within us.

From the poem *Dear Nusrat Fateh Ali Khan*
by award-winning poet Cyril Wong, from his
collection *Like A Seed With Its Singular Purpose*

The Legend of Badang

Badang was a poor but clever fellow who was originally from a rustic village up the Johor River. He made his home along the banks of Singapore River in the mid-14th century, surviving by trapping fish there. A run-in with a half man-half fish genie who had been stealing his fish led to Badang acquiring super-human strength. With his hard-earned strength, Badang caught the attention of the King who dwelled in Fort Canning Hill, and Badang was made a Royal Prince.

He then beat an Indian competitor by throwing a heavy stone from Fort Canning Hill all the way to the mouth of the Singapore River, and thus won seven ships full of treasures for Singapore. The spot from which Badang launched that stone is called "Badang Terrace" today, and overlooks Clarke Quay. It is fittingly outfitted with a fitness station, a more banal way to build muscles than an encounter with a genie.

1 Singapore Stone.

2 Amazing Badang! by Lat.

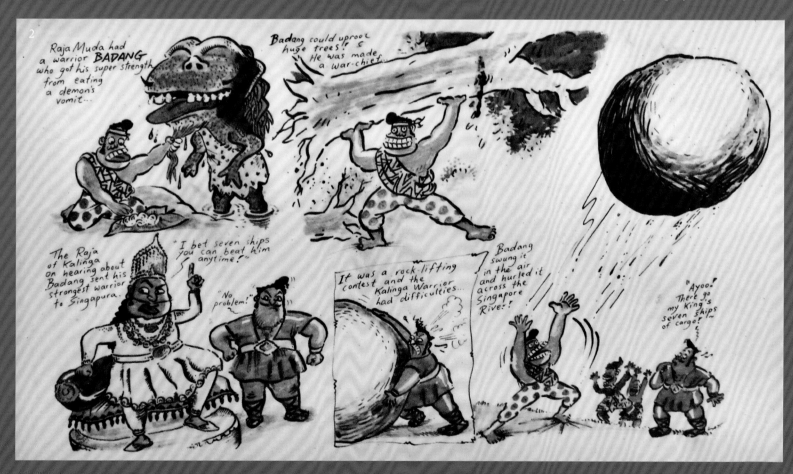

Faces and Phases: The Changing Names of the Hill

Bukit Larangan or Forbidden Hill

Pre-colonial (before 1819)
Graves of ancient Malay kings, stories of wandering spirits, a legendary forbidden spring that was used by ancient princesses or consorts on the hill and being out of bounds for commoners gave the hill the name Bukit Larangan or Forbidden Hill.

The hill, with its unfriendly reputation, was not known to have visitors until Raffles founded Singapore in 1819.

Singapore Hill

1819 to 1822
The hill became known as Singapore Hill from the time Raffles arrived in Singapore to the time he chose to build a residence on the top of the hill notwithstanding the mystery surrounding Bukit Larangan. In 1822 Raffles ordered that the forests around the hill be cleared, deciding to take command of the island from the hill. It was a practical choice for a cooler residence in a tropical country.

Government Hill, Flag Hill, Sir Bonham Hill

1822 to 1858
From 1822 to 1858 the hill took on various roles and names that reflected these as well.

Government Hill
Singapore Hill became known as Government Hill from 1822, when Raffles chose to build a wooden Malay style house on Singapore Hill. At that point, Singapore had few cool spots and this place provided the best views and cool breeze. Subsequently the Governor's residence was established on this hill.

Bukit Bendera or Flag Hill
The flagstaff communicated to the town below the arrival of ships and became the reference point that earned the hill the name Bukit Bendera (Flag Hill).

Bukit Tuan Bonham or Sir Bonham Hill
Named after Sir Samuel George Bonham, who was the Resident Councillor from 1822 to 1836, and then the Governor from 1837 to 1843.

Fort Canning Hill

1859 onwards
The Governor's residence was demolished to make way for a fort that was built in 1859 to protect the interests of the European community in Singapore. Once the military moved in, the name changed to Fort Canning Hill, after Viscount John Charles Canning, Governor-General and the first Viceroy of India.

1 Welcome to Fort Canning Hill, by artist Clara Wong.

2 The hilltop flagstaff in 1828, by Marianne James.

Twins Separated at Birth?

Singapore has Fort Canning Hill, and Mexico City has Chapultepec Park. Sitting atop Chapultepec Hill, this green lung overlooks the vast city. Over the centuries, both hills have had much in common.

1 Military College in the castle atop Chapultepec Hill, c. 1847, by Nathaniel Currier.

2 Fort Canning upon its hill, c. 1900.

Chapultepec Park	Fort Canning Hill
Toltec altar, 9th – 11th c	(Presumed) Malay shrine, 14th c
Aztec rulers' ashes burial, 14th-16th c	Malay king(s) burial, 14th c
Springs: fresh water, baths, aqueducts, Aztecs, 14th-16th c	Spring: fresh water, baths, moat (Malay, 14th c), and wells, aqueduct (colonial, 19th c)
Reserved for Aztec nobility, 14th – 16th c	Reserved for Malay nobility, 14th c
Gardens with trees and plants from across the empire, Moctezuma II, early 16th c	Royal fruit gardens (Malay, 14th c), Botanic & Experimental Garden (colonial, 19th c)
Site of one of last stands of Aztecs against Spanish, 1521	Last Malay king fled during a Majapahit invasion, 1401
Government residence (castle), home of heads of state, 18th – 20th c	Government House, home of heads of state, 19th c
Military academy in the castle, 19th c	Singapore Command and Staff College in (today's) Hotel Fort Canning, 1970-1976
Castle becomes a museum, 20th c	Art installations, galleries, and WWII museum (Battle Box) 21st c

The cupolas on Fort Canning Green, by artist Benedick Lim.

Benedick Lim
1 Mar 2012

Fort Canning

HERITAGE

Overview

Fort Canning Hill has always played a central role in all aspects of Singapore's heritage. Whether one is looking for Singapore's tangible cultural elements (such as buildings, ruins, art works, or landscape) or its intangible elements (such as folklore, historical knowledge, fleeting biodiversity, or inspirations), one's path inevitably leads to this hill.

During both ancient and colonial times, the hill has been the site for the seat of power. It has been instrumental in the island's trading economy. It has had military aspirations. It has housed the dead, who witnessed this all. Eventually, it was able to let down its defences and evolve into a place of relaxation, a place to help the public gain awareness and appreciation of their heritage.

Today is it a guardian of Singapore's unique – and irreplaceable – heritage.

1 Surrounding greenery reflected in the windows of the modern-day Raffles House, which sits roughly at the same spot as the original.

2 The Singapore River with Thomson Bridge, c. 1849-1853 by artist Edwin Augustus Porcher and engraver Vincent Brooks.

Military Heritage

New kingdom, old lines

When the Sumatran Prince Sang Nila Utama founded Singapore in 1299, he chose a hill overlooking a bustling river port as the site for his palace. That hill, of course, was Fort Canning Hill.

Sang Nila Utama's own Sumatran Srivijayan kingdom had been eclipsed by the Javanese Majapahit kingdom during the 13th century. Anticipating that outsiders might be interested in his new kingdom, he fortified the palace with a wall, as we learn from the 17th century *Serajah Melayu*, or Malay Annals.

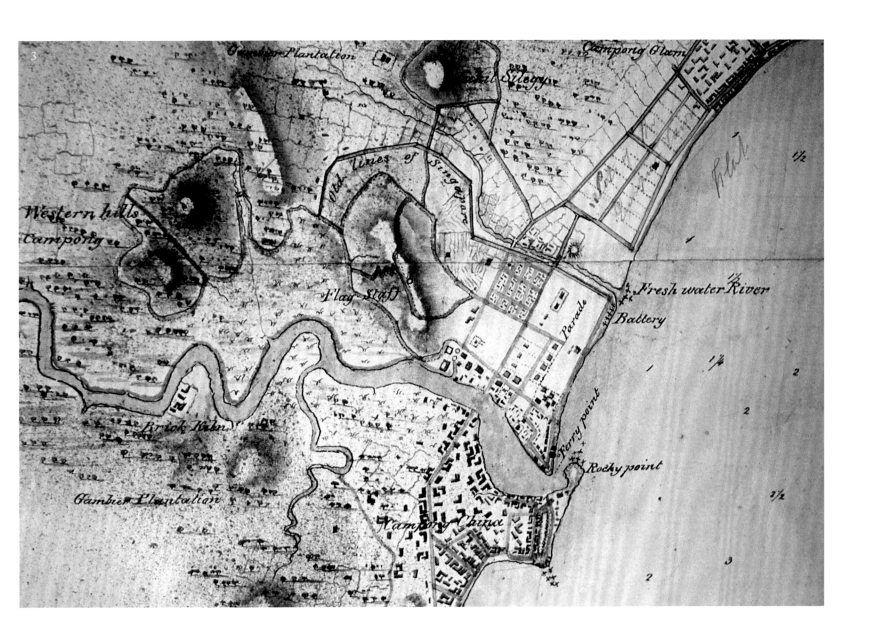

1 1925 view of Fort Canning entrance with sentry on guard.

2 Defending Singapura from behind its walls, designed by Eng Siak Loy, carved by Villa Frangipani.

3 Map from 1825, showing the wall remnants, called the "Old Lines".

Evidence of that wall was found many years later, in 1822. John Crawfurd, the future Resident of Singapore, found the ruins of a massive earthen rampart, nearly 5 m wide and 3 m high. The wall, dubbed the "Old Lines', ran for over a kilometre – all the way from Fort Canning Hill to the sea, which at that time was near the Padang. The hilltop palace and temples were thus protected by the wall along the North, by the sea along the East, and by the river's swamps along the South.

Contemporary evidence of the wall's necessity comes from Chinese merchant Wang Da Yuan's 1349 chronicles, *Essential notes on Foreign Lands*. He recounts that shortly before his 1330 trip to Singapore, the Siamese had attacked the city. The populace successfully closed its gates and managed to withstand the month-long attack.

During excavations at the top of the hill in 1928, several solid gold ornaments were unearthed. These "Kala head" armband and rings were probably hidden in the ground during a 14th century battle, and attest to the power and richness of the palace.

Another indication of the protection afforded by the fortified palace also comes from Wang Da Yuan. He wrote that ships arriving in Singapore first had to run the gauntlet of Dragon's Tooth Straits (leading to today's Keppel Harbor), which was full of bloodthirsty pirates, before they could attain the safety of the river port at the foot of Fort Canning Hill.

Bathing princesses and buried kings

The 14th century saw the Javanese Majapahit and the Siamese Ayutthaya kingdoms constantly battling for hegemony in the region. At times, they both claimed Singapore as a vassal. When the last of the 14th century kings of Singapura, Parameswara, murdered his predecessor (who was a Thai vassal), he was obliged to flee town following a Siamese attack to avenge the murder.

With the departure of Parameswara from Fort Canning Hill in 1396, the hill reverted to nature. While the kings were there, the hill had been off limits to the rest of the population. The presence of royalty, bathing princesses, temples, and buried kings resulted in the hill becoming "Bukit Larangan", or the Forbidden Hill. Even after the kings fled, this aura was maintained.

It remained a commercial and military presence throughout the 15th century (it was the base for the Melaka Sultanate's Laksamana, or naval leader, and *orang laut* warriors), the 16th century (the Portuguese attacked it, and battled the Sumatran Acehnese off its coasts), and the 17th century (the Portuguese attacked and burned the settlement). But no leader was to return to Fort Canning Hill until Sir Stamford Raffles christened it Government Hill in 1822.

1 The hill harboured riches worth hiding!

2 The pirates' cove at the Dragon's Tooth Straits.

3 Bathing princesses, by Lat.

4 Parameswara fleeing, designed by Eng Siak Loy, carved by Villa Frangipani.

Treaties and spices

Singapore reappeared from relative obscurity with the 1819 arrival of Raffles. He made a treaty with the Tengku Hussein (Prince of Riau) and the Temenggong (Governor of Johor) granting trading rights to the British East India Company. Though the British were late entrants as colonial powers in Southeast Asia, they wanted to expand their sphere of influence in the region, and established Singapore as a key trading post in their rivalry with the Dutch.

Both countries then built military strength and strategies aimed at supporting their growth. With the signing of the Anglo-Dutch Treaty in 1824, this rivalry "cooled" a little, and allowed the colonial powers to develop trade instead. Incidentally, one of the treaty's British signatories happened to be named Canning - not the hill's namesake, but a future Prime Minister nonetheless.

Negotiations leading to the signing of this landmark treaty spanned several years and various thorny issues were addressed. Some of these related to the British occupation of Dutch colonial properties, and trading rights for the Spice Islands. British subjects, for example, were given trade access to the Banda Islands, the original source of nutmeg, which was the only spice to become an economic success in Singapore. (Singapore's nutmeg trees had arrived indirectly via Sumatra.)

Ultimately, the Dutch opted for an exchange in which they laid claim to colonies west of the Strait of Malacca and south of the Straits of Singapore, and abandoned their claims on colonies to the north of the Straits of Singapore, which included Singapore.

1 Nutmeg and mace.

2 1900 view of Boat Quay, a centre of trade.

3 Peaceful cannon.

4 An Indian sepoy in the British army by Dhruv Angresh.

Secret societies and sepoys

Initially, Fort Canning Hill charmed the British with its height of about 48 m above surrounding areas, and a beautiful view from the top of the hill. Raffles, as well as subsequent governors, resided on the top of the hill, enjoying the cooler air and the panoramic views of the harbour.

Soon however, the colonial power perceived internal, as well as external threats and in 1859, decided to fortify the hill in order to use it for defence if the need arose. Among the internal threats was rebellion from the Chinese secret societies.

Chinese secret societies were initially set up as self-help guilds or associations to support immigrants of one or more particular dialects. These self-help organisations were legitimate, with the earliest and the biggest formed in 1820. However, soon rivalries emerged among the various societies.

As time went by, these societies became more powerful, and starting with the right to collect taxes and monopolise trade, moved on to become involved in opium smuggling, coolie brokering, brothels, gambling, extortion and murder. By 1850, the societies were the cause of riots and rebellion even against some colonial governing policies, such as a more expensive monopoly on post and remittances.

Singapore. Boat Quay.

When the British fortified the hill, they also needed to provide accommodation for the Indian soldiers, or Sepoys, transferred to Singapore. Upon the first Sepoys' arrival with Raffles in 1819, the military garrison had initially set up camp at the foot of the Fort Canning Hill. With the 1859 fortifications, new barracks were planned for the Sepoy regiment on a 70-acre site at Tanglin.

While this internal threat loomed, the British also faced the external threat of possible attack from sea, for which it was deemed important to be prepared.

So, in 1859, the Government Residence on the top of the hill was demolished, seven acres of land were cleared, and a fort was built on the top of the hill. Around 400 coolies levelled three hectares of hilltop to build an elaborate fort complex that included an artillery fort, a stockade with an arms store, barrack blocks, and a hospital.

The new fort was named after Viscount Charles Canning, who was then the first Viceroy of India. By 1867, the fort perhaps stored seven 68-pounder guns, eight 8-inch guns, two 13-inch mortars and a few 14-pounder cannonades - none of which were ever to fire for war.

The construction of the fort marked the beginning of a new military role for Fort Canning Hill, one which would evolve over time but not end until over a century later.

A fort, but no fights

The decision to build a fort on the hill was questioned by some leaders of the colonial power, who felt it was a mistake to build a fort so far from the shore. Some residents wrote in to the newspapers also expressing similar views. True enough, this distance did put the cannons and guns at Fort Canning at a disadvantage against enemy ships at sea, and ultimately the fort was never used in the defence of the city, but more as a signal station.

2 IT is said that Her Majesty's Government intend fortifying Singapore, and making it the Gibraltar of the "Far East.' It is to be hoped that the fortifications to be built will be something different from Fort Canning–built on the ruined reputation of suckling Engineers. Every Military man of note who has visited this Settlement, has condemned it as utterly useless.

Raffles himself, however, seemed to be in favour of building a fort on 'Government Hill', and one of his 1819 letters to the first Resident of colonial Singapore, William Farquhar, includes this recommendation: "...On the hill overlooking the Settlement, and commanding it and a considerable portion of the anchorage, a small Fort, capable of mounting 8 or 10 pounders and of containing a magazine of brick or stone, together with a barrack for the permanent residence of 30 European artillery, and of temporary accommodation of the rest of the garrison in case of emergency."

When Fort Canning was completed in 1861, it was discovered that the neighbouring Pearl's Hill was 4 m higher than the fort, and stood in the line of the guns mounted at Fort Canning. The Government Military Engineer ordered that Pearl's Hill be shaved off to meet the right height.

Till 1896, the cannons were fired to signal time, to signal the outbreak of fires in the town, and possibly to remind everyone in town where the seat of power was. In the early 20th century, the hill was essentially used as a communication centre aided by a flag staff, a time-ball, a lighthouse and a telegraph office.

1 Reminders of the fort that once dominated the hilltop, by artist Clara Wong.

2 A useless fort? Excerpt from *The Straits Times* on 16 March 1861, p. 1.

3 19th century barracks at Fort Canning.

4 1925 view of bunker at Fort Canning.

Marching into the 20th century

The fort was decommissioned in 1907 but not demolished until 1926, to make way for a reservoir where the large artillery barracks and parade ground were located. The Gothic archway gate entrance (the Old Fort Gateway, 1859), designed by G. C. Collyer, some remnants of the fort wall, and the Sally Port are all that remain today.

The disappearance of the fort, however, did not spell the end of the military presence on the hill. That same year, the British army constructed barracks that now form Fort Canning Centre, a space for performing arts, park administration, and venue spaces.

In 1926, the British Far East Command Headquarters also built an imposing administration building on the northern slope. During the Japanese Occupation of World War II, the building housed the Japanese military. From the end of the war until Singapore's independence from Britain in 1963, it was the seat of the British Military Administration. The 4th Malayan Infantry Brigade then moved in, only to be replaced by the Singapore Armed Forces upon Singapore's separation from Malaysia.

In its last military incarnation, the building was used for the Singapore Command and Staff College from 1970 to 1976. Nearly 20 years of disuse followed before the edifice finally transitioned to a peaceful role. The end of the 20th and start of the 21st centuries saw it being transformed sequentially into the Fort Canning Country Club, the Legends at Fort Canning, and finally today's Hotel Fort Canning.

During the Japanese Occupation that followed, the headquarters of the much-feared Japanese military police force, the Kempeitai, was in the YMCA building at the northeastern base of Fort Canning Hill. This beautiful Art Deco building (from 1911), witnessed ruthless interrogations, torture, and imprisonment of countless civilians. For years after the war, the building inspired shivers of horror in Singaporeans who had lived through the Occupation, with some passersby swearing that they could hear the ghosts of the dead still screaming. Finally, nearly 20 years after the end of the occupation, those memories were erased when the original building was razed and a new one was built on the same spot.

Behind Hotel Fort Canning, an old gate opens onto Dobbie Rise. A commander leaving the Command Headquarters would only have to pass through this gate to enter the underground bunker across the road. The bunker, built in 1936, became part of the Malayan Command Headquarters during World War II. Today a museum called the Battle Box commemorates this as the place where Lieutenant-General Percival signed the British surrender of Singapore to the Japanese forces in February 1942.

1 The fort's well-camouflaged Sally Port.

2 Battle Box diorama of the signing of the surrender.

3 The original YMCA in 1923.

Cannons and cannonballs

In the heyday of the fort, there were over a dozen cannons strategically positioned around the hill. However, none of them was ever called into action. Today, two 9-pound cannons ceremonially "hold the fort", although "9-pounders" were obsolete by the time the fort was built in the mid-19th century and came from an earlier fortification elsewhere.

The main battery of guns was located behind a brick wall around the Raffles Terrace area, and consisted of seven massive "68 pounders". The decorative 9-pounder near Raffles' House is located in one of the original cannon positions. When the fort existed, a cannon located here would have been aimed at Middle Road, about 1 km away, well within the gun's range. At the time, the sea came up to Beach Road, so any invading ships dropping anchor in the deep water off of Middle Road would have been targets.

As their name implies, these cannons would have fired cannonballs that weighed 9 pounds (about 4 kg) or 68 pounds (31 kg). Those balls are no longer kept at Fort Canning Hill, although there is another type of cannonball there. This kind weighs only 1-2 kg, and has a range of about 1 m – it falls only to the base of its tree, the spectacular Cannonball tree (*Couroupita guianensis*).

The fast-growing Cannonball tree is a native of Central and tropical South America, and is related to the Brazil Nut tree. Its eye-catching trunk can be covered year-round by the unique cannonballs and elaborate crimson flowers.

4 The beautiful flower of the cannonball tree.

5 A peaceful cannon, by artist Jason Tay.

6 "Cannonball" close-up.

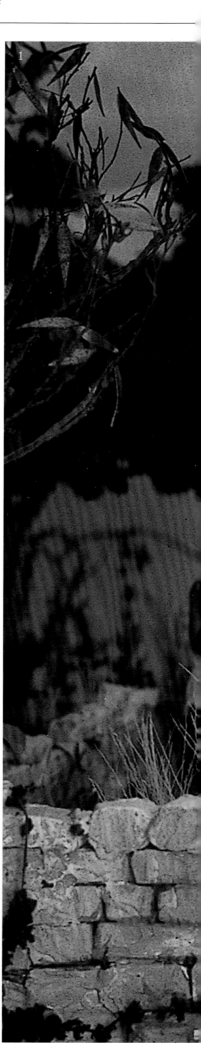

Architectural Heritage

The expanse of green in Fort Canning Hill is like a canvas that various artists have contributed in creating. These include botanists, architects, theatre artists, sculptors, and even military leaders.

The result is an interesting masterpiece collage dotted by remnants of varied construction activity through time starting from the 14th century.

Ruins and royal styles

In ancient pre-colonial times, the style of architecture was known to be influenced by the culture and religion of the surrounding region; therefore the classical Hindu, Buddhist and Islamic styles were popular around this region as well.

Soon after ascending the hill, the British discovered stone foundations and extensive ruins of brick buildings from the north and east sides of the hill. Holes discovered in the foundations might have supported a wooden superstructure. In accordance with the prevailing style of 14th century, the palace, fort or temple that existed could have used sandstone and featured terraces too. These structures certainly attest to an important presence on the hill, in a time when the rest of the town's buildings would have been of wood and palm thatch. Interestingly, this ancient palace would have faced east as did all regional palaces of the time and Raffles' first house on the hill.

Archaeological digs around the summit of the hill reinforced the theory of the existence of a Malay Palace there. The most imposing of the former buildings stood on a terrace roughly where the *keramat* is today. This *keramat* features a 14th-century-styled 'Pendopo' (Malay roof) supported by twenty wood pillars carved in a fighting cock motif of Javanese origin. *Keramat* means "sacred place" in Malay and traditionally, it is a burial ground of a revered leader. It is not known for certain who, if anyone, is buried at Fort Canning, but some believe it houses the tomb of Sultan Iskandar Shah, the last ruler of Temasek (ancient Singapore), while others dispute that since Iskandar Shah supposedly died in Melaka.

1 Ruins of ancient settlement on Fort Canning, 1823.

2 The *keramat*.

Historic Inspiration for Speculative Fiction

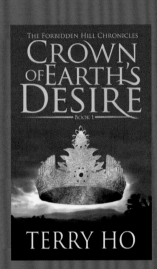

The archaeological dig one can visit on the hill has stimulated one Singaporean author of speculative fiction. A university student researching the island's pre-colonial history has received a ominous note in the middle of the night:

"We have kidnapped Miss Clarissa Lee. If you want to see her alive again, meet us as the archaeological dig site at Fort Canning at 6.45 a.m. tomorrow. We will discuss terms then. Speak to the police, and Miss Lee's life is forfeit."

Source: "Crown of Earth's Desire", the first volume in The Forbidden Hill Chronicles book series by Terry Ho. Courtesy of Renaissance Publishing.

Civil impressions

On the establishment of a British Settlement here in 1820, architecture took on a largely colonial style. However, initially, Irish architect George Coleman designed a simple wooden bungalow as a residence for Raffles and his sister's family. It was 100 ft long and 50 ft wide, with venetians and a roof made of *attap* (leaves of the Nipah Palm, *Nypa fruticans*). It had two parallel halls with verandahs at both the front and back and two square wings that served as sleeping quarters. This was later converted to the Governor's residence, giving the name 'Government Hill' to Fort Canning Hill.

When the Governor's residence was demolished to make way for the fort, a new residence was built on Mount Caroline in the Palladian style. This is what we know as the Istana today.

Currently, the structure at Raffles Terrace in the heart of Fort Canning Hill is near the spot where Raffles chose to build his first residence. The views of the city around have evolved with time, but are still as captivating as they were known to be in earlier days.

The black-and-white bungalow was a common architectural style used to build houses for expatriate families in 19th century British tropical colonies. The building style incorporated elements of Art Deco as well as English Arts and Crafts. The homes were airy and large enough to accommodate affluent families. They were usually painted white with black accents and today, they are accompanied by mature foliage around that lends a beautiful scenic feel to the buildings.

A charming old black-and-white bungalow from way back in 1908 that used to be the former residence of the Fire Chief has been converted into a contemporary fine dining restaurant. The Fire Chief's Retreat and the open wood deck verandah are the two options available for seating.

Did the imposing gates at the entrance of Fort Canning Green's expanse arrest your attention? These were Singapore's earliest structures in Gothic-Revival style. Later, the St Andrew's Cathedral and Chapel of the Convent of the Holy Infant Jesus were also constructed in this style.

The Fort Canning Gothic Gates were designed in 1846 as the gateway to the Christian Cemetery which existed until 1865 where the open green expanse of the park now stands. The gates were designed by the Superintendent engineer in the colonial government, Captain Charles Edward Faber, and bear the words 'IHS' above both gates. IHS stands for "Iota Eta Sigma", the first three letters of the Greek word for Jesus.

1 Raffles Terrace.

2 The former Fire Chief's house, now a restaurant.

3 One of the Gothic Gates.

Military imprint

The preserved ruins of the original 1860 fort wall and the adjoining gates are remnants of the fort. The construction of the wall began in 1859 even while the Governor lived in his residence on the other side of the hill towards current-day Raffles Terrace.

The exterior wall of the fort was made of granite. It had an earthen filling and the interior was made of bricks. This was planned more to absorb the shocks of cannon ball bombardment rather than an infantry soldier attack. The wall was also surrounded by a moat, which no longer exists.

A Sally Port, which is a concealed exit meant to allow undetected escape from a fort, also exists on Fort Canning. Currently, you can go up the remaining Sally Port, the only one of the original three to have survived.

Though a lot of the physical structure of Fort Canning has been changed over time, remnants of the park's military past are still visible in classical buildings like the recently-restored Hotel Fort Canning. It is a three-storey neo-classical style building that was previously used as a military administration building in 1926. In its current state, the details in the building reflect its rich colonial legacy and the hotel has been awarded Singapore's Urban Redevelopment Authority's Architectural Heritage Award.

British Army barracks were added in 1926 as well. These have been restored as Fort Canning Centre. Over the years, the centre has provided space for National Parks Board offices, the performing arts, events, and art exhibits.

1 Fort Gate, by artist Kit Madula.

2 The former British Army barracks, today Fort Canning Centre.

following page The former British Far East Command Headquarters, today the Hotel Fort Canning.

4-14-12
FORT CANNING GATE
9:30 AM

'KIT'

At the foot of the hill

Hill Street had a variant Chinese nickname, Ong Ke Sioa Kha, which meant "foot of the Governor's hill'. At the foot of this hill are two captivating buildings.

One, with the colorful window shutters at the corner of Hill Street and River Valley Road, is the Old Hill Street Police Station. The station was constructed in 1934 to accommodate offices, garages, and living quarters for 125 married as well as 144 single policemen. The building was built in the classical Renaissance style with blocks arranged around two courtyards. A part of the slope of Fort Canning Hill was excavated by rock blasting to accommodate the needs of the building towards the rear. The building is a gazetted National Monument and currently houses the headquarters of the Ministry of Information, Communication and the Arts.

The other interesting building at the foot of the hill is the Central Fire Station, which was gazetted as a National Monument in 1998. The building is built in the early Edwardian 'Blood and Bandage' style, using two-toned bricks in red and white for the facade. It was completed in 1909 and is Singapore's oldest functioning fire station. It houses a heritage gallery showcasing firefighting history in Singapore as well.

Find them around Fort Canning:

- Neo-classical style: Hotel Fort Canning, Fort Canning Centre

- Gothic-Revival style: Fort Canning Gothic Gates at the entrance to the Fort Canning Green

- Colonial military style: Sally Port, Fort Gate

- Javanese style: Keramat

- Early Edwardian 'Blood and Bandage' style: Central Fire Station

- Classical Renaissance style: Old Hill Street Police Station (formerly known as MICA building)

- Black-and-white style: Flutes at the Fort

1

1 The Old Hill Street Police Station was built in 1934.

2 The Central Fire Station, by artist Rey Villegas

3 Fireman ready for action.

Trading Heritage

Regional trade in ancient times

Singapore is ideally situated for maritime commerce: The Indian Ocean, the Indonesian archipelago, and the seas of the Far East have all been busily crisscrossed by trading vessels for many centuries. The Singapore River has served as the hub for most of this activity.

The neighbourhood of Fort Canning Hill has always been intimately involved in trading. Archaeological digs on its slopes have unearthed pottery from Thailand and China, as well as glass beads and coins from China, evidence of the dynamism of the river's port. The riches of the kings of the 14th century were partially due to these international commercial activities.

As the Chinese explorer Wang Da Yuan wrote in 1330: "The goods used in trading are green cotton stuff, pieces of iron, native cotton prints, dark red gold, porcelain ware, iron pots, and such like things." Items traded by the Chinese were "red gold, blue satin, cotton prints, Quzhou-fu porcelain, iron caldrons".

1 14th century glass beads from China. Over 10,000 of them were found on Fort Canning Hill.

2 A Yuan Dynasty bowl made between 1328 and 1352, depicting a traditional motif of ducks and water plants.

3 14th Chinese century stoneware jar, probably from Guangdong.

4 Trading during Singapore's Golden Age, 1300-1400, designed by Eng Siak Loy, carved by Villa Frangipani.

Port activity and the hill's help

From the vantage point of Fort Canning Hill, it was possible to have an eye on just about everything going on in the town, along the Singapore River, and in the ocean harbours. The hill became instrumental in passing on the information it gleaned from the harbour to the rest of the settlement.

1 View of the seafront from Fort Canning.

2 Map of the town and environs of Singapore, drawn by J.B. Tassin from an actual survey by G.D. Coleman, Calcutta, 1836.

3 Archaeology Professor John Miksic and his team placing 19th century local and British artefacts at one of Hotel Fort Canning's lobby archaeological pits.

4 1861 view of flagstaff from the busy harbour, by artist W. Gray and lithographer W.H. McFarlene

Large ships would drop anchor in the estuary at the Singapore River's mouth, and along the coast to the east until the Kallang River. Before land reclamation, the sea came up to the Padang, and the beach was literally along Beach Road, which housed godowns to receive goods from the ships.

By 1825, a flagstaff sat atop Fort Canning Hill. In port cities the world over, flagstaffs were were used to communicate with their towns. In Singapore, the flagstaff was diligently used to display the arrival, identity, location and status of the ships entering the harbour. This included signalling the exciting and much awaited arrival of a ship with mail. The red ensign signalled closing of mail for Europe, a blue ensign for Calcutta, a white one for Australia, and a yellow one for China. The hill began to be called Bukit Bendera or Flag Hill in the latter part of the 19th century for this reason. The current flagstaff is not the original, which was of wood and much taller.

The flags hoisted provided information of the type of cargo being carried, the ship's last port of call as well as the people on board. With the information provided, merchants could rush to the harbour to be the first to buy - and bargain for - goods. Flags could also be used to communicate with the ships in the harbour. The top of the hill also featured a lighthouse to guide the ships.

Those ships were impressively numerous, and were coming to Singapore from the East and West. They stopped at Singapore, as a final destination as an entrepôt stop, or to replenish fresh water, food, and coal (for steamships, starting in the 1860s). With the opening of the Suez Canal in 1869, 800 km were cut off from a journey between Asia and Europe, leading to even more shipping traffic.

The heavy maritime traffic of the early 19th century

In 1820, Farquhar wrote that there were "upwards of 20 junks, 3 of which are from China, 2 from Cochin India, the rest from Siam and other vessels are at anchor", and 1840 a British sailor recounted: "Before the town, and at a distance of a mile from it, lay numerous huge junks, all glittering with white and red and green eyes ... Within these junks were thousands of prahus [smaller traditional boats] of every size and form, stretching away into a narrow and shoal harbour which lies to the right of the town." (from the article "Tales of the Old Orient", by S.C. George, in *The Straits Times*, 3 April 1949).

Early on, the need for a new maritime port was anticipated. Coleman was responsible for laying roads across the swampy area from Tanjong Pagar to Telok Blangah to prepare for the new port. Mid-century, "New Harbour" was located at today's Keppel Harbour to take advantage of the deep water. There was a constant flow of goods between the docks of New Harbour and the godowns of the Singapore River, below Fort Canning Hill. A system of steam trams was put into place to transport cargo from New Harbour all the way to Boat Quay.

The Singapore River did not have adequate berthing facilities for ocean-crossing ships. Instead, their cargo was transferred to large *tongkangs* (or bumboats) that could easily go up the river to the quays. These boats had to wait for low tide to be able to fit under certain bridges. The river area adjacent to Fort Canning Hill developed rapidly throughout the 19th century.

1 View of Cavenagh Bridge with tongkangs and twakows at the Singapore River at low tide.

2 Modern day Boat Quay.

After Raffles' arrival, gambier and pepper plantations increased dramatically, as did the Chinese Teochew merchants' (or *towkays*) trading houses along the river quays. Two of the most successful gambier traders were Seah Eu Chin (1805-1883) and Tan Yeok Nee (1827-1902). Along with his warehouse (near Read Bridge), two of Tan's residences are still standing today: River House (now the Forbidden City restaurant on Clarke Quay) and the University of Chicago Booth School of Business (at the corner of Clemenceau Avenue and Penang Road) are both gems built in the Southern Chinese architectural style.

Throughout the 1830s, all ships visiting Singapore would replenish their freshwater stocks at Clarke Quay with water from the formerly "forbidden" spring. By the end of the century, the river - from Boat Quay to beyond Robertson Quay - was home to innumerable godowns (warehouses), villages, mills, and boatyards. Read Bridge was a hub for trading fuel - wood, charcoal, and oil - imported from Melaka. The hustle and bustle of the river's shores was a huge contrast with the serene and stately homes of the wealthy – who often made their fortunes in the trading houses – elsewhere in Singapore.

From railroad station to MRT station

Did you know that at one point the western boundary of Fort Canning Hill was the Singapore-Kranji railway?

The Tank Road to Bukit Timah section opened on New Year's Day, 1903:

"Yesterday morning at 6 o'clock sharp, the first train drew up at the platform awaiting those daring spirits who had decided to test the line, in an initial run as far as Bukit Timah. There were 2 or 3 Europeans, and a similar number of Chinese babas as passengers", read an article in *The Straits Times* that appeared the very next day.

Water from a tank filled from Fort Canning's "forbidden" spring probably served to fill the steam locomotives' own tanks. Although the line was extended to Woodlands within a few months, the Tank Road station remained the only station where passengers could board until the Tanjong Pagar station was completed 20 years later. Sundays were particularly busy at the station, with gamblers going up to Johor's gambling "farms", whose owners encouraged the traffic by paying for the return leg of the gamblers' trips! Many of the Hindu Chettiars who frequented Sri Thendayuthapani temple, next to the station, also appreciated the ease with which they could travel to their businesses around Malaya.

A few years later, the railway was extended to the Pasir Panjang docks, allowing it to transport freight. This finally brought to fruition a plan discussed since the 1860s, to link the Malayan railway with Singapore's "New Harbour" (Keppel Harbour). Malayan commodities (e.g., tin, rubber, pepper, gambier) were primarily shipped out through Singapore's port. Transporting these goods by railway for the entire journey was an obvious logistical advantage.

The station was abandoned once the Tanjong Pagar passenger station opened, and the Tank Road to Bukit Timah line was dismantled on the eve of World War II.

Today, a little over a century after the railroad station opened, a new station for the Mass Rapid Transit station is under construction. Fort Canning Station, to be station number 20 on the new Downtown Line, will be following in the footsteps of its charming predecessor.

1 Tank Road station in 1903.

2 1921 map of Singapore showing the Tank Road area railway.

3 Artist's rendition of the MRT station across from Fort Canning Hill.

A Heritage Cemetery

Graves and tombstones

Of intrigue there is plenty on Fort Canning Hill.

Even before the British set foot on it, the hill housed a tomb that was tended by local Malays. It was believed to be the grave of the last ruler of ancient Singapore, Iskandar Shah, who ruled Singapore for around 50 years. However, since he fled to Melaka during a Siamese attack, it is debated whether he is actually buried there. The *keramat* (a Muslim shrine) there is dedicated to Iskandar Shah, and it is well tended and revered. Occasionally, it is possible to spot someone paying respects at the shrine even these days.

left A wall of tombstones.

1 1900 view from Fort Canning of the cemetery and the town beyond.

2 The tomb at the *keramat*.

For the first few years of the British settlement, the area near the top of the hill was used by the Europeans as a burial ground. When Raffles built his residence near there, the cemetery was too close for comfort. The original Christian cemetery was thus closed and a new cemetery was opened on another part of the hill. The register of lands issued by Raffles and John Crawfurd, second Resident of Singapore, lists this as 'lot 576, burial ground on Government Hill - 2 acres'. This was the part where Fort Canning Green stands today. The new cemetery was used from 1822 to 1865 but only consecrated in October of 1834.

Though the site was marked for Protestant and Catholic burials, no real distinction was followed as such since it was such a small piece of land. The cemetery was extended in 1845 and a brick wall was added to enclose the entire cemetery. The next year in 1846 the Gothic Gates were added as well. These were designed by Government Engineer Captain Charles Edward Faber. The brick wall and the beautiful and imposing gates stand at the entrance to the Fort Canning Green even now.

Around 600 burials took place in the Fort Canning Cemetery, with one third of these Chinese Christians. Gradually the cemetery became full and was officially closed in 1865. Although no more burials were allowed after that, there was one exception in 1868 when special permission was granted for a Marie Scott whose parents also rested in the cemetery on Fort Canning Hill.

Over time, the graves and the cemetery deteriorated. There were some efforts for a cleanup and a few graves were personally tended, but generally, the ravages of time changed the face of the grounds. Many of the gravestones became illegible, and in addition, the official burial register of the cemetery was lost.

In 1912, the government hired a clerk to survey and compile a report of all burials and map the graves that existed then on Fort Canning, preserving much of the information we have today. In 1952, an article appeared in *The Straits Times* highlighting that new plans were underway for the oldest Christian cemetery in Singapore.

'History is written in these dying stones'

The Straits Times, 23 September 1952, by Francis Wong

66 At the age of 130 years, this historic burial place is gradually disappearing....A few headstones have sunk entirely into the ground; on all of them the **epitaphs** have been worn illegible or completely obliterated; over some, ants have built their nests....

The process of deterioration has advanced beyond repair. But though Fort Canning Cemetery as a graveyard is doomed to disappear, there is a project afoot to preserve the actual site and its historic value.

The government has authorised the Singapore Committee for the preservation of historic sites to convert the ancient churchyard into the colony's newest park. The process of conversion however will be a slow one. It has been decided to allow the decaying headstones to collapse in their own time and to use them to build a perimeter wall around the new park. So far only a score of fallen headstones have been collected. Each month however the Public Works Department visits the cemetery to look for others. 99

By 1954, the government had decided to convert the entire hill into a park. The gravestones that could still be salvaged were embedded into the brick wall that had surrounded the cemetery in order to preserve them. This is where they rest currently, telling poignant tales of lives led by people who lived in the 19th century.

Sociological snapshots

On the wall, gravestones of John Collingwood from the ship 'Susan', and a judge visiting from India are from 1821, and previously rested in the original cemetery near Raffles Terrace.

Other tombstones, which speak of young deaths, bring these times to life. A good proportion of the buried are infants, toddlers and young wives. Many more are young men who were struck down in the prime of their lives.

1 1925 view of the cemetery.

2 Tombstones on Fort Canning Green, moved here from the old Bukit Timah cemetery, by artist Tia Boon Sim.

3 A boy's tombstone.

One 'grave' blogger discovered some interesting stories connecting people in different countries. Fort Canning has the gravestones of the wives of two missionaries whose own graves are elsewhere. The first is Mary Gutzlaff, the wife of Karl Gutzlaff who is buried in Hong Kong. Another is Matilda Dean, the first wife of William Dean. His second wife, Theodosia, is buried in Hong Kong. William himself is buried in Rochester, New York.

There are a few prominent burials among the graves, and these include George Coleman, the first Government Architect of colonial Singapore. The panel in the wall comes from his original tomb, which was a large structure resembling that of the Napier memorial.

Coleman was responsible for the construction of some iconic buildings in Singapore including the Armenian Church and the old Parliament House (currently The Arts House). He died in 1844, and his widow later married William Napier, Singapore's first law agent. They had a son together, but the little boy, James Brooke Napier, died in infancy. A big memorial was erected in Fort Canning in the little boy's memory and stands preserved in the corner of the green expanse until today.

Other burials of notable personalities include Charles Spottiswoode, a British merchant, Aristakes Sarkies who was an Armenian merchant, and Captain William Scott, cousin of Sir Walter Scott, and Sir Jose D'Almeida Carvalho, the Portuguese Consul-General and one of the earliest European merchants in Singapore, and his family. All of these people are recognisable in Singapore as there are roads here named after them.

On the other corner of the green is a group of 12 gravestones which were not original burials at Fort Canning, but which were removed and placed here from the old Bukit Timah Cemetery when it was converted into a park in 1971. These include the gravestone of William Cuppage, who was the acting Postmaster General around the 1840s, and original owner of the area that is now Emerald Hill.

1 Coleman's tombstone.

2 Napier memorial and the cupolas, on Fort Canning Green, by artist Pocholo Estremos

Margaret Trudeau - the string that ties Singapore to Canada

Digging up their roots fascinates many people these days. Although not buried in Fort Canning, the name of Major General William Farquhar, first Resident of colonial Singapore, throws up an interesting link. William Farquhar is credited with establishing Singapore as a bustling port and his commissioning of local artists to draw the flora and fauna of the region has greatly helped the understanding of Natural History at that time.

Margaret Trudeau, the ex-wife of former Canadian Prime Minister Pierre Trudeau, always knew of an 'Indian Princess' lineage that was a part of her family legend. She spent time researching at the Singapore National Library, National Museum of Singapore, and the National Archives. Along with meetings and help from professors from the National University of Singapore, archivists and curators, she discovered she is indeed the great, great, great, great granddaughter of William Farquhar, the first Resident of Singapore. Farquhar had married Antoinette Clement, the daughter of a French officer and a Malaysian woman. Esther, the eldest of their six children, married British officer Francis James Bernhard. Esther was Margaret Trudeau's great, great, great grandmother.

Botanic Heritage

Fruit fit for a king

Before there was any king of the hill, Fort Canning Hill was covered with the same dryland forest that covered the rest of the island. But when the 14th century kings converted the hill to their private gated community, they needed to clear some of the forest away. They also terraced the slopes, allowing fruit trees to be planted.

Gardens with fruit trees were an integral part of most palaces in the region at that time. John Crawfurd, who would become second Resident, presumed that the fruit trees he encountered were descendants of those planted by the kings centuries ago. He remarked in his journal in 1822: "Here we find the durian, the rambutan, the *duku*, the shaddock (pomelo), and the other fruit trees of great size: and all are so degenerated, except for the 1st two, that the fruit is scarcely to be recognised." Which is exactly what one would expect, if no one had been maintaining and selecting the trees for over 400 years!

Botanic & Experimental Garden: a first try

Raffles came to Singapore to in order to develop a trading post on behalf of the British East India Company. One of his missions, therefore, was to explore the possibilities for cultivation of crops of economic importance such as nutmeg and cacao. Immediately upon his return to Bencoolen after his first brief stay in Singapore, he sent a gardener back to Singapore along with nutmeg trees and seeds and clove trees. These were planted in the small Government Garden on the hill, in 1819.

But Raffles was also a serious botanist, and interested in the science – and not just the economy – of plants. His work on the botany of Java and Sumatra had already garnered admiration from the British Royal Society. So when Dr. Nathaniel Wallich, the Superintendent of the Calcutta Botanic Gardens, proposed a more extensive and scientifically ambitious garden, Raffles knew he had found a kindred spirit and supported him wholeheartedly.

They were both familiar with the botanic gardens of Europe, and of their evolution over the centuries: medicinal plant gardens first, then showcases for the exotic plants arriving during the Age of Exploration, then cultivation of some of these for economic reasons. The granddaddy of them all, the Botanical Garden of Padua (Italy) has been inscribed on the list of UNESCO World Heritage Sites, as it "represents the birth of science, of scientific exchanges, and understanding of the relationship between nature and culture". Modern words, but only expressing what Raffles and Wallich already appreciated, and perhaps hoped to replicate. As Raffles wrote to Wallich, "it is hardly possible to conceive a position [Singapore, in the heart of the Malay archipelago] more admirably calculated for such an establishment as your active zeal in the Cause of Science has prompted you to suggest".

Thus, in 1822, the Botanic & Experimental Garden was established, encompassing the original Government Gardens. The increased land (19 ha) was filled with a much greater diversity of plants, including gambier, pepper, sugar cane, coffee, tea, and several other tropical spices and crops. In addition, part of the hill was transformed into a park, a predecessor of the current beautiful park.

1 Durian, the king of fruits.

2 Rambutan bronze plaque along the sidewalk of Orchard Road.

3 Nutmeg and mace.

4 Cloves.

5 Pepper.

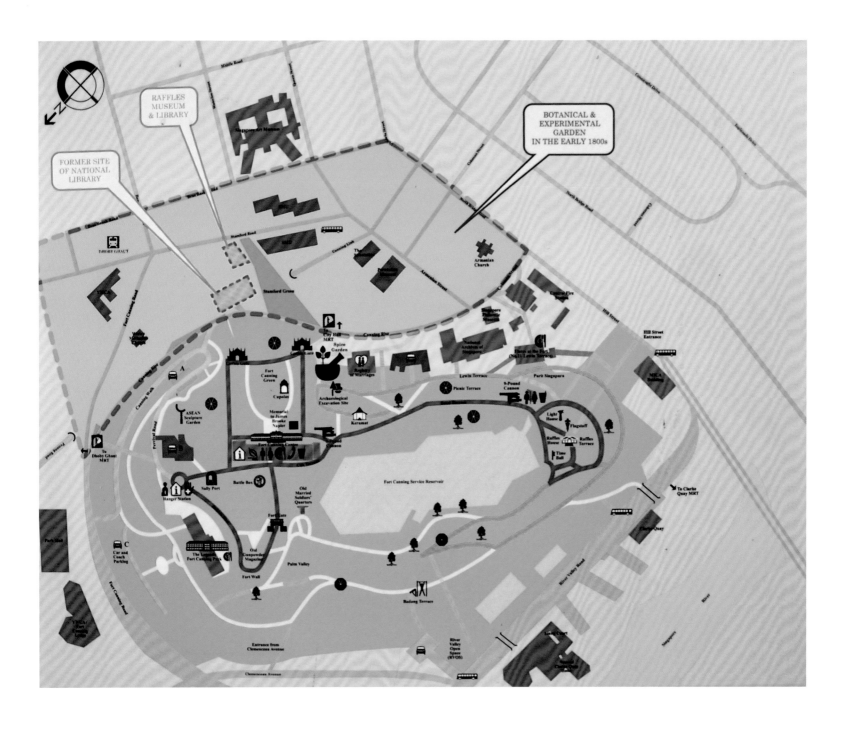

above The extent of Raffles' Botanic & Experimental Garden.

This happy state of affairs was not to last. Raffles died in 1826, without a champion to his botanical cause. By 1829, the garden no longer had the government funding needed for maintenance and a director. Ten convicts took partial care of it, until 1836 when the civilian Agricultural and Horticultural Society revived a diminished 2.8 ha version of the gardens. This too was temporary, until finally in 1859 the government transferred the gardens to a new 24 ha site in Tanglin, which later became the Singapore Botanic Gardens.

Spice garden: a fresh aroma

In 1994, years after the Botanic Gardens had decamped to their current Tanglin site, a small Spice Garden was planted in Fort Canning Hill, to be a much-reduced version of the original gardens. This 0.23 ha (2300 m sq) of land contains a good number of nutmeg trees and a couple of clove and coffee trees, all species that were planted in the original gardens. There are also many plants important in local cuisine - such as pandan, various varieties of ginger, lemongrass, curry, laksa, turmeric, cardamom, starfruit and belimbing trees.

1 to 5 Ginger roots, cacao, cloves, cinnamon bark and vanilla beans.

The heritage trees of Fort Canning Hill

When we think of Singapore as our Garden City, it is partially due to the majestic, mature trees that grace the landscape. To encourage us to preserve these special trees, the National Parks Board started the Heritage Tree Scheme. Heritage Trees are particularly outstanding trees, for any of several reasons, such as trunk girth, rarity of species, age, and historical, cultural, or social significance. They must not be cut down or have their roots injured, of course, and are protected from lightning.

Fort Canning Hill is home to 11 Heritage Trees:
• 4 Madras Thorns, *Pithecellobium dulce*
• 2 Ear-pod trees, *Enterolobium cyclocarpum*
• 2 Sea Beams, *Maranthes corymbosa*
• 1 Flame of the Forest, *Delonix regia*
• 1 Rain Tree, *Samanea saman*
• 1 Terap, *Artocarpus elasticus*

1 Madras Thorn tree (*Pithecellobium dulce*), branches.

2 Ear-pod tree (*Enterolobium cyclocarpum*) seed pod. It's easy to understand why Earpod Trees are thus called!

3 Sea Beam tree (*Maranthes corymbosa*).

4 Flame of the Forest tree (*Delonix regia*).

5 Rain Tree (*Samanea saman*), branches.

6 Rain Tree (*Samanea saman*), flowers.

7 Fruit of the Terap (*Artocarpus elasticus*).

Precious nutmeg

On the sidewalk beside the Ion Orchard retail mall, sits a lone nutmeg – a striking, huge, bronze nutmeg that surely baffles most passers-by. Little do they realise that the nutmeg sits there because of Fort Canning Hill!

Coveted in Europe from the Middle Ages onward, the nutmeg (*Myristica fragrans*) hails from the tiny Banda Islands in eastern Indonesia. Europeans were obliged to purchase it from Arab traders, who kept its source a trade secret.

Finally, in the early 16th century, the Melaka-conquering Portuguese learned of its origin, and were able to eliminate the Arabian middlemen. By the early 17th century, after a bloody war on the Banda islanders, the nutmeg trade had been wrested away by the Dutch. So lucrative was this spice trade that the Dutch and English spent part of the century fighting over it.

When the English finally took over the trade in early 19th century, they planted nutmeg trees in other colonies. Raffles arranged for 125 nutmeg trees and 1,000 nutmeg seeds from Bencoolen (Sumatra) to be planted on Government Hill. Of all the crops that were tried, none was as successful in Singapore's soil and climate as nutmeg. By the 1830s, the high market value of nutmeg led to a race by Europeans and Chinese to plant trees, which are not very productive until they are about 15 years old. The nutmegs were so valuable that people were fined for illegal picking.

Today, the Spice Garden at Fort Canning Hill sports about two dozen nutmeg trees. But back during Singapore's nutmeg craze, some plantations had over 5,000 trees, and could extend over 40 hectares. By 1848, there were 24 plantations containing a whopping 56,000 trees. The Dempsey-to-Orchard area in particular was crawling with nutmeg plantations.

The heyday of this trade was short-lived. By the early 1860's, cultivation ended due to a combination of dropping global nutmeg prices and a blight that killed most of the trees. The useless plantations were sold off. Europeans and wealthy Chinese merchants left the central part of the city to build luxurious "suburban" homes on the land. The Mount Harriet (today's Dempsey Hill) nutmeg estate was sold to the government, which constructed the Tanglin Barracks that are still in use.

1 "Nutmeg", by Kumari Nahappan.

2 A nutmeg on its tree.

Orchard Road area roads that are named after nutmeg planters:

- Cairnhill Road: In the mid-1840s, Charles Carnie had a nutmeg plantation and a home on "Carnie's Hill".

- Cuppage Road: William Cuppage once owned a nutmeg plantation on the hill and surrounding area.

- Grange Road: Colony surgeon Dr. Thomas Oxley bought a massive area of jungle in 1837, and transformed it into a nutmeg plantation. Grange Road was built as a private pathway to his home, Grange House.

- Killiney Road: Dr. Oxley named his nutmeg plantation Killiney Estate.

- Oxley Road: This runs down the middle of Dr. Oxley's estate, which was bounded by Orchard Road, Leonie Hill, River Valley Road and Tank Road.

- Prinsep Street: Charles Prinsep's nutmeg plantation, surrounding today's Selegie Road, harvested 22,000 nutmegs per day! In 1867, over 100 acres of the estate was purchased for a new government building – the Istana.

- Scotts Road: William Scott owned Claymore nutmeg plantation.

3 Traditional English dessert recipe from *Herbes to season, herbes to cure* by Grace Acton (1621).

4 The chemical structure of myristicin.

What on earth were the Europeans doing with all that nutmeg? Since the Middle Ages, nutmeg was used to preserve and flavour food, such as porridge, meats, pickled foods, cakes, and even wine. The 1861 best-selling "Mrs. Beeton's Book of Household Management" included mace and nutmeg in nearly all of the potted fish and meat recipes.

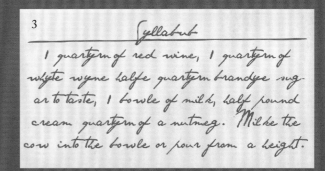

3

Syllabub

1 quartern of red wine, 1 quartern of whyte wyne halfe quartern brandye sugar to taste, 1 bowle of milk, half pound cream quartern of a nutmeg. Milke the cow into the bowle or pour from a height.

In Shakespeare's plague-ridden times, people thought that nutmeg (often mixed into wine) could protect against plague, which increased its value. Nutmeg, mace, and other "exotic" spices were recommended for a host of ailments. In the early 18th century, nutmeg, cardamom, ginger, galangal, and cinnamon went into "Dr. Stephens Water", which "comforts ye spirits, helps cold desentes, old coughs, women in travail, dropsy, wormes, give 3 spoonfulls of ye best at any time, the weakest to children."

At the time that Raffles was planting his garden, it was believed that large doses of nutmeg could induce abortion, which did not lead to many successful abortions but did lead to many cases of nutmeg poisoning in women. The famous Czech physiologist Purkinje deliberately overdosed on nutmeg in an 1829 experiment, and had headaches and hallucinations lasting for several days. Nutmeg oil contains many compounds, some of which inhibit prostaglandin production (as do many painkillers), or inhibit monoamine oxidase (as do some anti-depressants), or are psychoactive.

A LIVING PARK

Overview

Fort Canning Hill is historically significant. It is located within the Civic District, and is often included in heritage-themed tours.

And yet, Fort Canning Hill is far from a relic and continues to evolve and be used in perpetually "modern" ways. Concerts and art exhibitions are held here, and there's also an award-winning hotel.

Everyday, the hill's trees shade runners and *tai chi* practitioners from the equatorial sun. On the weekends, families picnic where once kings plucked fruit from their royal gardens. Fort Canning Hill is the home to majestic trees and languid butterflies. It is a vibrant, living park.

1 Life in the park.

2 Symphony of green.

3 Saga tree seeds.

Natural History

Fort Canning Hill harboured a natural, wooded ecosystem until the 14th century kings transformed some of it for their use. During the 400 years following their departure, the ecosystem had time to recover at least partially. Since most of the jungle surrounding the hill had not been cleared, there was still a "reservoir" of plants and animals that could re-populate the hill.

The hill (like the rest of the island) was almost completely denuded during the colonial period, and stayed that way until the 1930s, as we see from this 1947 article in *The Straits Times*:

"10 years ago the land at the junction of River Valley Road and Tank Road was an abandoned railway goods yard, and the slope of Fort Canning Hill behind it was entirely bare."

Yet today, it is a lush oasis of trees in Singapore's bustling downtown.

That is wonderful, and is due to impressive forethought from several municipal authorities over the past 75 years. However, while we should rejoice in this fertile green space, what exists now on our hill is a completely managed habitat, with low biological diversity. Nearly every plant in the park was deliberately placed there by human hands. (The animals, as animals will, came mostly of their own volition.)

In this section of the book, we highlight some of the more captivating of those animals and plants.

Artful *Artocarpus*

It is easy to spot the similarities among the fruits of the breadfruit, jackfruit, cempedak, and even the Terap trees, all members of the *Artocarpus* genus. But it is less easy to see their similarity to figs, or amazingly, mulberries! Yet they all merrily reside within the family Moraceae: They bear "compound" fruits, formed from a cluster of flowers that mature into a single fruit, and secrete a milky latex sap when wounded.

Originating in Southeast Asia, the *Artocarpus* genus includes about 60 species of trees. Three of those are found on Fort Canning Hill. The majestic Terap can grow to 45 m tall, and sports beautiful bark and striking, large leaves. Breadfruit trees seduce our eyes with their gorgeous leaves, while jackfruit trees tempt our tongues with the fruity sweetness of their enormous fruits. Jackfruit, in fact, was likely one of the varieties of trees planted on the hill when it was the seat of the 14th century kings.

In addition to eating their fruits and building with their timber, traditionally, people have made use of *Artocarpus* tree bark to make rope and clothing, and to line baskets. Although their latex is much more dilute than that of the rubber tree, it has been used to trap birds and caulk boats.

1 Terap tree (*Artocarpus elasticus*).

2 Jackfruit tree (*Artocarpus heterophyllus*).

3 Breadfruit leaves

Dominating dipterocarps

When the earliest British colonists took in the view of Singapore's skyline from Fort Canning Hill, they would have been struck by the crowns of the giant dipterocarp trees, towering over the rest of the forest canopy. These long-lived, majestic trees are a characteristic component of Asian tropical rainforests. They are named after their distinctive fruits, which resemble badminton shuttlecocks with two to five wings ("di ptero" = two wings, and "carp" = fruit). Their dense wood is hard and strong, attributes that led to them being chopped down for timber. Today, dipterocarp trees are naturally found only in the Central Catchment and Bukit Timah Nature Reserves.

Fort Canning Hill, however, has been planted with two species of these trees that were so important in the island's early economy:

- *Hopea odorata*, better known as Chengal pasir or Ironwood, is an evergreen tree with a conical shaped crown that can attain 40 m in height. Its fruits have two long and three short wings, to help their dispersal by the wind.

- At nearly 20 years of age, the *Shorea sumatrana*, or Sengkawang at Fort Canning are still saplings. Sengkawang fruits have greatly-reduced wings (making them resemble miniature mangosteens), which are designed for dispersal by water – this species is often located along riverbanks.

Yet, you may not spot any of their unique fruits beneath these trees. That is because the trees generally only fruit once every few years. But when one dipterocarp tree in an area fruits, almost all of them do, using a strategy called "mast fruiting". The ground is so covered with nutritious oil-rich seeds, that whatever predators (e.g., beetles, rats, birds, pigs) there are cannot possibly eat them all up. And so the surviving seeds go on to develop into seedlings.

3 The characteristic winged fruits of *Hopea*.

4 *Hopea odorata*, or Chengal Pasir.

5 *Shorea sumatrana*, or Sengkawang.

Fascinating *Ficus*

In tropical forests, fruit from fig trees is an abundant resource that is found nearly all year long, supporting many animals. They are so important in sustaining animal populations that they are considered "keystone" species. The fig trees at Fort Canning Hill provide food for birds, bats, and rodents. Three of the most common species in the park are the Common Red-Stem Fig (*Ficus variegata*), Malayan Banyan (*Ficus microcarpa*), and the Benjamin Fig (*Ficus benjamina*).

Like jackfruit and breadfruit trees, they bear compound fruits, which are actually fleshy structures containing male and/or female flowers inside.

And, they could just as easily be called "wasp trees" as "fig trees".

1 The climbing fig *F. aurantiacea* and its abundant fruit.

opposite page Common Red-stem Fig and its abundant fruit.

following page Banyan tree arch over Dobbie Rise.

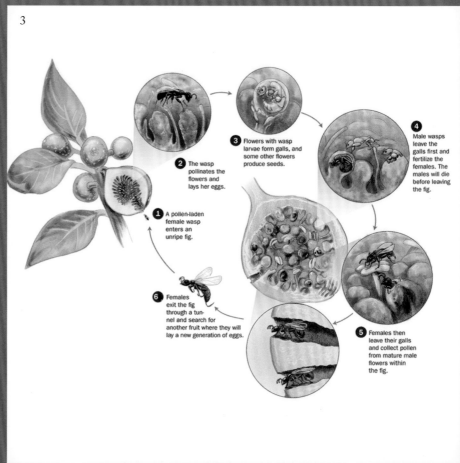

Figs and fig wasps

What happens inside those figs is nothing short of amazing.

There are three kinds of tiny flowers inside a fig fruit: male, "short female", and "long female" flowers.

A minuscule female fig wasp (in the family Agaonidae) arrives at an unripe fig, and forces her way in through a very narrow opening at the fig's bottom. Once she enters, she inserts her tube-like ovipositor into the female flowers, trying to lay her eggs at their base. But she only manages to reach the bottom of the short flowers. Thus, only in the short female flowers will eggs be deposited and baby wasps develop.

As she crawls around inside the fig trying to lay her eggs, she also deposits the male pollen that she earlier picked up from the male flowers within her own birth fig. This pollen fertilises the female flowers. Thus, only the eggless long female flowers will develop into fig seeds.

Then, after laying her eggs the female wasp dies.

When her daughters grow up, they escape from their birth fig, fly to another unripe fig, crawl in, and start the cycle all over again. Their wingless brothers, on the other hand, are not so lucky. Their jobs are to mate with their sisters within their birth fig, chew a hole so that the sisters can leave the fig, and then unceremoniously drop dead.

Thus, the figs are dependant on the wasps to pollinate them, and the wasps are dependent on the figs for shelter and food for their babies. This system is a perfect example of "plant-insect mutualism".

1 Delicate female fig wasps.

2 A pollinating wasp entering a native *Ficus fistulosa* fig.

3 The fig and fig wasp life cycle.

Strangler figs

Fort Canning Hill is home to many "strangler" figs. For these trees, it is not the fig fruits that attract our attention, but rather their aerial roots and web of "branches". You have only to look at the majestic Malayan Banyan tree overlooking the Fitness Station, or the two solemn Benjamin Fig trees on the grassy plateau next to Fort Gate, to be amazed by these trees.

Fig-eating birds or other animals drop off the seeds of the strangler figs on branches of different trees, high above the ground. The little fig seedling grows, and when big enough it sends down long roots that reach the ground, while the rest of the tree grows up towards the light.

Strangler figs come from tropical and sub-tropical forests, where the dense forest canopy lets little sunlight reach the ground. By starting their lives high in the branches, they do not have to compete for light with other tree seedlings.

Eventually, as the fig tree grows and wraps itself around its host tree, it blocks too much of the sunlight and takes up too much of the nutrients in the ground. Biting the hand that feeds it, the strangler fig kills its host tree, and a hollow area forms in the midst of the fig roots. Macabre, alright.

1 Not hard to see why they're called "strangler" figs!

2 Malayan Banyan.

3 A tree you can see through, because its host tree is gone!

Fort survivor!

If you were to find yourself magically trapped on Fort Canning Hill, with all the restaurants closed and no way to escape – well, you might get lonely, but you would NEVER get hungry! (We will pretend that you have access to a stove, oil, and salt.) You can follow the recipe at the end, or get your own creative juices going and devise your own recipe.

Is it time for dinner? Here are some of the ingredients in your pantry:
• Breadfruit (*Artocarpus altilis*), as your starch
• Candlenuts (*Aleurites moluccana*), to thicken your curry sauce
• Jackfruit (*Artocarpus heterophyllus*), unripe fruit and seeds, as another starch
• Petai beans (*Parkia speciosa*), for flavoring (no garlic on the hill) and protein
• Four-angled beans (*Psophocarpus tetragonolobus*), for protein and crunch

To jazz them up, you could rummage through the Spice Garden and add, to taste:
• Chili peppers (*Capsieum frutescens*)
• Clove buds (*Syzygium aromaticum*)
• Curry leaves (*Murraya koenigii*)
• Ginger root (*Zingiber officinale*)
• Laksa leaves (*Persicaria hydropiper*)
• Lengkuas root (*Alpinia galanga*)
• Torch ginger flower (*Etlingera elatior*)
• Turmeric root (*Curcuma longa*)

Feeling peckish in the afternoon? Prepare some snacks:
• Jackfruit seeds (*Artocarpus heterophyllus*) – just boil the seeds from the ripe fruit
• Melinjo (*Gnetum gnemon*) – pound and fry the kernels to make "emping" chips

1 Lost in the jungle!

2 Stone balustrade.

Then when dessert rolls around, invent a delicious fruit salad using:
- Bananas (*Musa* spp.),
- Belimbing (*Averrhoa bilimbi*)
- Jackfruit (*Artocarpus heterophyllus*)
- Pineapple (*Ananas comosus*)
- Water apple, or Jambu air (*Syzygium aqueum*)
- Starfruit (*Averrhoa carambola*)
- And a dash of nutmeg (*Myristica fragrans*).

And don't forget to brew yourself a nice cup of coffee (*Coffea* spp.), and make it something special with a stick of cinnamon bark (*Cinnamomum verum*) or a grating of cocoa bean (*Theobroma cacao*).

Or perhaps you don't want the caffeine. Then try a refreshing infusion of lemongrass (*Cymbopogon citratus*) and pandan (*Pandanus amaryllifolius*) leaves.

If the mosquitoes become too pesky in the evening, tear off some citronella (*Cymbopogon nardus*) leaves and spread their juice on your skin – no harsh chemicals, you will smell great, and most of the mosquitoes will leave you alone.

If you are at a loss to devise your own recipe, here is some help:

Thick Breadfruit Curry
- Pound a handful of candlenuts until you get a paste.
- In your pan add a tablespoon of oil, a little chopped ginger (a one-inch piece will do nicely), a little chopped turmeric root (again a one-inch piece will do), the candlenut paste, and 2 clove buds.
- Once this starts to brown, add a handful of curry leaves, the chopped breadfruit and salt to taste.
- Roast this for a minute or two, and then add a cupful of water.
- Cover the pan and let this boil for 20 minutes on reduced flame or till the breadfruit is cooked.

Eat it hot, with a side dish of winged beans stir-fried with petai beans, chili and salt to taste.

Lastly, chew on a betel pepper leaf (*Piper betle*) for fresh breath till you are rescued!

2

Nuts about betel!

Betel *nuts*? Not really. The Betel pepper plant does not have nuts, but its *leaves* are used to wrap up the *nut* of the Areca palm.

What exactly was in those betel nut quids so popular with the Peranakans in days of yore?

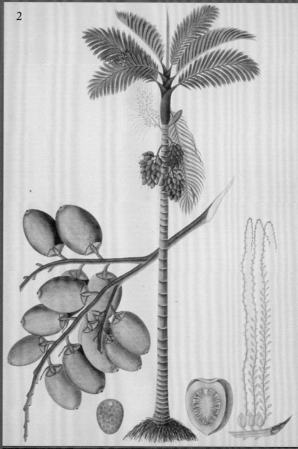

Areca palm nuts

What is used: The dried fruit of the palm, cut into small pieces.

What it provided: A feeling of mild euphoria, due to the nut's major active ingredient, a stimulating alkaloid called arecoline. The addictive nut is also the carcinogenic part of the quid, and is the fourth most used drug in the world (nicotine, ethanol, and caffeine are the 1st, 2nd & 3rd).

1 Betel nut quid

2 Betel nut palm (*Areca catechu*).

3 Bits of Areca palm nut.

Slaked lime

What it is: Calcium hydroxide, $Ca(OH)_2$

Source:

- Limestone, coral and seashells contain calcium carbonate [$CaCO_3$].

- Grind them up and heat their calcium carbonate to produce calcium oxide [CaO]:
  $CaCO_3 \rightarrow CaO + CO_2$.

- Mix this calcium oxide with water to form "slaked lime", which is calcium hydroxide [$Ca(OH)_2$]:
  $CaO + H_2O \rightarrow Ca(OH)_2$

What it provided: The lime helps release the alkaloids from the palm nut, so that they can be better absorbed.

Gambier

What is used: The leaves of the Gambier shrub were boiled, and the extract made into a paste.

What it provided: Flavouring

Gambier was hugely important for the development of Singapore in the 19th century. When Raffles landed in 1819, there were already 20 gambier and black pepper (generally grown together) plantations, and some gambier plants were also grown in the Botanic & Experimental Garden on the hill.

A member of the coffee family, gambier and its tannin-extract had multiple uses: As a medicine, cloth dye, leather tanning agent. By 1848, gambier and pepper together accounted for 76% of the total acreage and 61% of the total agricultural gross revenue. While lucrative, gambier cultivation had a devastating effect on Singapore's ecosystem: by the end of the 19th century, 90% of the jungle had been cleared.

4 Slaked Lime.

5 Gambier (*Uncaria gambir*).

Betel pepper

What is used: The leaves

What it provided: A spicy-peppery wrapper, which contains chavibetol, a spicy phenylpropanoid compound.

Betel nut set

Betel nut chewing (*makan sireh*) was a popular social pastime among the Malays and Peranakans. Offering betel nuts on an attractive betel nut set (*tempat sireh*) was an important Baba custom when guests were entertained.

Gambier extract was mixed with lime, and the paste smeared on a betel leaf. Pieces of areca palm nut were added, and then the leaf was rolled into a little packet, or quid.

1 Betel pepper (*Piper betle*).

2 to **4** Components of the betel nut set: nut cutter, slaked lime pot, betel receptacle.

Rooted to the hill

A noticeable feature of numerous trees in Fort Canning Hill is their trunk "buttresses". The Terap (*Artocarpus elasticus*) trees, in particular, have strikingly beautiful buttresses, and the park's young dipterocarp (see section "Dominating dipterocarps") *Shorea* already has well-developed buttresses.

These organic architectural elements are common in rainforests. They make sense for several reasons, which all impinge on one raison d'être: to stabilise a tall tree with shallow roots growing in slippery soil. You can think of buttress roots as insurance against catastrophe.

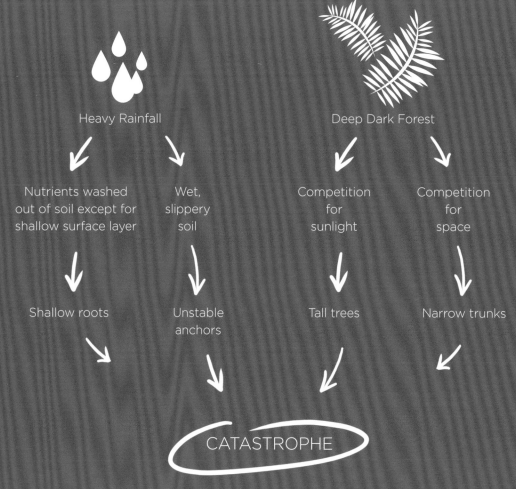

Heavy Rainfall		Deep Dark Forest	
Nutrients washed out of soil except for shallow surface layer	Wet, slippery soil	Competition for sunlight	Competition for space
Shallow roots	Unstable anchors	Tall trees	Narrow trunks

CATASTROPHE

above Terap buttress roots.

When is a tree not a tree?

When it harbours an entire ecosystem: Epiphytes (mosses, orchids, ferns, fig tree saplings), and insects, and snakes, and rodents, and bats.

Most of the large trees in Fort Canning Hill that have rough spongy bark are covered with veritable gardens of epiphytic ferns. Epiphytes are not parasites; they steal only real estate from their tree hosts, using them as a support for their seeds and spores to germinate and grow. The sheer weight of ferns on a tree can be a considerable structural stress, however. A study of redwood trees living in a temperate rain forest found up to 740 kg of fern mats on individual trees!

The most common epiphytic ferns in the park are the Bird's Nest Fern (*Asplenium nidus*), the Staghorn Fern (*Platycerium coronarium*), the Ribbon Fern (*Ophioglossum pendulum*, which often grows out of an Staghorn Fern), the Dragon's Scales Fern (*Pyrrosia piloselloides*), the Oak Leaf Fern (*Drynaria quercifolia*), and the Rabbit's Foot Fern (*Davallia denticulata*).

1 Is there a tree in there?

2 Ferns, ferns, ferns.

3 Bird's Nest Fern, seen from below.

The ferns drink the rainwater caught in the bark, as well as among their own dead leaves. That damp, rotting leaf litter also provides nutrients for them. The larger ferns (Staghorn Fern, Bird's Nest Fern) can provide a proper microenvironment for smaller species (e.g., Adder's Tongue Fern). They can also provide a refuge for animals, some of whom could not survive in a drier, non-epiphyte, environment such as reptiles, insects, and even bats.

In the air

Butterflies

"Bring back the colourful dancers!" exhorts a panel in the garden of the nearby National Museum of Singapore. That garden, across the road from Fort Canning Green, is located at one end of the Butterfly Trail, which begins 4 km away at the Singapore Botanic Gardens.

Stamford Green has been planted with hundreds of host and nectar plants to do just that. Butterfly caterpillars are more finicky eaters than even the most finicky child: If they don't find their favorite food, they will simply stop eating until they die.

The butterflies do not stay put on the Green, but also travel through Fort Canning Hill across the street. During the month or less of their adult life, they bring joy to park visitors young and old.

1 Blue Pansy (*Junonia orithya wallacei*).

2 A female Great Mormon (*Papilio memnon agenor*).

3 Tawny Coster (*Acraea violae*).

Dragonflies

Despite their name, they do not spew flames, but they *are* as old as the dragon-like dinosaurs. These modern-day flying fossils are ferocious predators, and their prey thankfully includes mosquitoes. Princess Pond, the small man-made pond above the River Valley and Clemenceau Roads intersection, is graced with these flitting jewels. Most of those jewels are males; the females come back to the water only for mating and egg-laying.

4 Blue Dasher (*Brachydiplax chalybea*).

5 Common Scarlet (*Crocothemis servilia*).

Bats

A tropical rainforest without its bats, why - that would be like Singapore without Changi airport: it would simply cease to function.

Bats, particularly fruit bats, or Megachiroptera, perform two tasks that keep the forest humming. They eat many fruits, such as figs, and subsequently disperse their seeds to propagate their trees. They also take over from the birds and the bees at night, and pollinate the flowers of many trees. Without bats, there would be no petai, kapok, wild banana, *Sonneratia* (an important mangrove tree), and, most importantly, no durian!

One can sometimes spy sleepy little Common Fruit Bats (*Cynopterus brachyotis*) hanging upside down in the shade of a tree or Birds Nest Fern. These park dwellers do not have to go far to find food since the park has at least one fig tree fruiting all the time. And there's always tart belimbing if the fig is too sweet.

Red Jungle Fowl

A century ago, the homes surrounding the park may have had chickens in their yards, and hearing a cock-a-doodle-doo would have been a common occurrence. But, whence come the cock-a-doodle-doos heard in today's park?

They come from the Red Jungle Fowls pecking about. Originating in Southeast Asia, they are still found in a few lucky spots in Singapore. These ancestors of the domestic chicken, whom they strongly resemble, are distinguished by their grey legs and by the males' white ear patch. While they spend their day foraging on the ground, they fly up into the trees to roost at night.

1 A trio of Red Jungle Fowl looking for a snack.

2 Fruit bat snoozing in a belimbing tree in the Spice Garden.

3 *Panthera leo* holding the fort.

On the ground

Changeable Lizard

Frequently encountered sunning themselves on the park's paths in the early morning, the Changeable Lizard (*Calotes versicolor*) was not seen in Singapore before the 1980s. Yet today it is the most common agamid lizard in town. These innocuous-looking lizards are actually aggressive invaders who have taken over urban gardens formerly belonging to the elegant Green Crested Lizard (*Bronchocela cristatella*).

4 Changeable lizard.

5 Green crested lizard.

6 Paradise Tree Snake.

7 Red ants "participating" in the BIG Feast sculpture by Joyce Loo.

following page Red Weaver Ants.

Paradise tree snake

Always come to the park armed with your camera, as you never know whom you may encounter. A Paradise Tree Snake (*Chrysopelea paradisi*) perhaps? Rarely, unless you have the eyes of an eagle. But its moulted skin, on the other hand, you may find draped over a branch at eye level.

With the pattern of its scales as intricate as Peranakan *nyonya* embroidered beadwork, this snake is an excellent tree climber. It can also glide by flattening its slim body and launching itself toward the next tree. As expected, it eats what it finds up in the trees, tree-dwelling lizards and small birds.

Red ants

They practically chase you down to bite you. They eat small cute furry (dead) animals. They use child labour. Who are these ruthless insects? They are the large red Weaver Ants (*Oecophylla smaragdina*), which keep you on the park's paths and away from tree trunks.

These ants, often seen in formation marching up a tree, "weave" together leaves to form a nest. They bind the leaves' edges together with silk, which they obtain by squeezing it out from one of their own children (larvae).

Their bites are so painful because those sharp mandibles are needed for gripping leaves and making short work of any small animal (such as mouse) carcasses they encounter - leaving only the white bones.

You may want to get even with the little devils by, well, by eating them, as some people do in several Asian countries. Lemony, it seems.

Water and the Hill

Over the ages, the relationship between Fort Canning Hill and water has been of primordial importance. A river, a spring, a moat, an aqueduct, and a reservoir – what more could a hill ask for?

Life along the Singapore River

The Singapore River, flowing along the southern base of the hill, was the centre of trading activity even before the glorious 14th century put Temasek on the map.

Picture the hubbub of goods from other Asian lands arriving along the swampy shores - pottery, porcelain, glass, and fabric. This activity continued on through subsequent years, peaking during the century of rule by the "5 Malay kings", then later declining until Raffles established a free port here.

Large ships were not able to navigate as far as Boat Quay and Clarke Quay. Smaller boats were necessary to ferry goods back and forth between the quays and the ships berthed in the harbour. Who was manning all those river boats in the 19th century? At first, the boats were large and the boatmen were Indian. Later, Chinese boatmen took over with their smaller boats that decreased the time to load and unload – these were the ancestors of the "bumboats" plying today's river.

In the early 19th century, gambier trading houses were located along the river, and remained there even after the plantations themselves moved out of Singapore. Godowns or warehouses also lined the shores of the bustling river. One unique godown was not only located on the shores of a water body, but it was also filled with water! Frozen water, that is. Hoo Ah Kay (1816-1860), aka Whampoa (after his birth place), was a brilliant and immensely wealthy man. He obtained the land for this godown in a swap for some land in his Tanglin plantations, later used for the Botanical Gardens when they moved out of the Fort Canning Hill area. Whampoa actually dared to import ice from the Kennebec River in the northeast United States. After a three-month journey, the ice would be stored in "Whampoa's Ice House". His business plan was overly optimistic and the venture eventually closed due to insufficient demand!

Forbidden hill, forbidden spring

When Prince Sang Nila Utama picked the top of Fort Canning Hill as the location to build his palace at the turn of the 14th century, he did so not only for the hill's view and river access, but importantly for the freshwater spring on its southwest side. That spring provided water used for drinking and for bathing.

Bathing places were important in palaces of this region, and their ruins exist to this day in Sumatra and Java. Thus, it is easy to give credence to the legend that the royal wives and princesses used the spring as a discrete bathing place, lending it its name of "Pancur Larangan", or Forbidden Spring – forbidden to all commoners.

And was that same freshwater spring used to fill the reservoir which gave its name to Tank Road in the 19th century?

The spring supplied all the fresh water needed by all the ships stopping in Singapore until 1830. An aqueduct was built to carry water from the spring to the riverside, where rowboats would fetch it and ferry it to the ships.

Ancient Chinese and Malay accounts tell of a protective moat on the east of the hill, the *Parit Singapura*. The source of the water for the moat was from Mount Sophia. While the moat has long since disappeared, it is thought to have run from the hill to Coleman Street, until reaching the sea by the Padang.

Throughout the 19th century, wells were dug around the base of the hill. Many of the wells were built as a public service by the Al-Juneid family, who had had a family home near the hill, on the corner of High Street and North Bridge Road. The wells, while undoubtedly useful, probably led to the mystical, life-giving spring finally drying up.

1 The busy river port in 1900.

2 A princess emerges from her bath, designed by Eng Siak Loy, carved by Villa Frangipani.

Fort Canning Service Reservoir

Where once soldiers had footraces and tug-of-war competitions, the very top of Fort Canning Hill has been occupied since 1926 by a service reservoir. At the time it was built, it was among the largest covered reservoirs in the world, and could hold two days' worth of the colony's water needs. Being a service reservoir, its water is pumped there from large impounding reservoirs. It was designed so that its hilltop location would allow the water to flow downhill for local use.

Its unusual design, with a honeycomb-like roof of hexagonal domes, includes foundations that extend 4.5 m below the original ground level – and whose excavation unearthed glittering 14th century gold jewellery stash, including the Kala armlet and rings.

Water for fun

Imagine an afternoon in the early 1960s. It's hot. You're bored. There's no television, and little extra cash. So what do you do today?

You could go to the base of Fort Canning Hill, along River Valley Road, where you would find the Van Kleef Aquarium and the River Valley Swimming Complex.

Van Kleef Aquarium

The aquarium, opened in 1955, was air-conditioned, soothingly dark, and affordable. Unique in Southeast Asia, it was also one of the most amazing aquaria in the entire world at that time. Its collections concentrated on Malayan fauna from various aquatic habitats – salt water, fresh water, and even coastal swamp water. All that made it so attractive that at its peak – 1979 – it hosted 430,000 visitors! Its curator, Alvin Fraser-Brunner, was not only a Fellow of the Zoological Society of London (which had been founded by Raffles), but he was also the designer of the Merlion emblem.

The unlikely source of the money for the aquarium construction and operation was an Indonesian-born, Dutch-Jewish businessman, Karel van Kleef. Van Kleef had lived – and prospered – in Singapore around the turn of the 20th century, and in his 1900 will, he bequeathed his entire estate to Singapore for the "embellishment" of the city.

He died in 1930, but the aquarium only opened in 1955 – what took so long? Firstly, there was the controversy over exactly how to embellish Singapore: a garden, or zoo, or circus, or broadcasting station, or drinking fountains, or clock towers, or aquarium? The Director of Fisheries convinced the committee that an aquarium would be both popular and profitable, and thus gained the funding.

Then, architectural plans, construction costs, and finally World War II got in the way. Later, there was more controversy, this time over the site selection. Fort Canning Hill allowed the water reservoirs to be located higher than the display tanks, eliminating pumping steps, and thus won.

For nearly 40 years, it maintained its popularity, and then in 1996 the ageing aquarium finally shut its doors and emptied its tanks.

River Valley Swimming Complex

Shortly after the end of World War II, when the site at the foot of the hill first had a park, an article in *The Straits Times* supported the addition of a pool to the park, yet had this to say about its clientele:

"...the city fathers should remember that the cleanest water which most of the youngsters of that neighbourhood ever swim in is the viscid blackness of the Singapore River, so their notions of hygiene in a public swimming pool are likely to call for a super-efficient chlorinating plant."

Nonetheless, those city fathers did open the River Valley Swimming Complex a decade later, in 1959. Located at the base of Fort Canning Hill, it soon became very popular. This public complex had both a wading pool and an Olympic-sized pool, for recreational use and for swimming lessons.

Children and adults would descend en masse on weekends to get relief from Singapore's humid weather. The title of a 1972 article from *The Straits Times*, "Getting all heated up in the long futile wait to cool off", was self-explanatory: So many people would show up (up to 1,000 each weekend afternoon) that some would have to be turned away in frustration. Meanwhile, those who did manage to enter certainly would not have had a lane to themselves!

After over 40 years of constant use, the facility was dilapidated, as well as less frequently used due to a population decrease in the neighbourhood. That, coupled with expiration of the Singapore Sports Council's lease, led to its closure in 2003. Today, it has been converted to The Foothills Fort Canning Park.

Princess Pond

Today, an artificial but nonetheless adorable pond greets visitors as they pant up the first set of stairs from River Valley Road. It is a calm little oasis full of tadpoles and frogs, dragonflies and reeds, which instantly provides respite after a weary climb.

1 The Fort Canning service reservoir

2 1950s view of the Van Kleef Aquarium.

3 The welcoming pool, with Fort Canning Hill as a backdrop.

The Arts

Theatres and thespians

Every July, scores of arts enthusiasts enjoy watching the Singapore Dance Theatre's "Ballet Under the Stars", while picnicking in Fort Canning Hill. Most of them do not realise that the hill was also the location of several theatres in the past.

Coleman House

George Coleman - surveyor, city planner, and Singapore's first architect - built his two-storey brick home across the road from the Fort Canning Hill's original Botanic & Experimental Garden. When Coleman left Singapore, he leased the house to Gaston Dutronquoy, who transformed the dining room into the Theatre Royal, which hosted the Settlement's amateur theatricals until 1845.

The actors who regularly performed included several whose names grace today's roads: William Napier (Singapore's first lawyer), Charles Spottiswoode (a merchant), and William Read (a businessman and magistrate famous for both his actor and actress roles).

How fitting it is that Spottiswoode and Coleman have their gravestones incorporated into the wall surrounding Fort Canning Green, as if they themselves are watching the performances today.

Assembly Rooms

In 1845, the Assembly Rooms were built at the foot of the hill, in a building "distinguished by its ugliness". It provided space for public functions, a free school, and the new Theatre Royal, complete with an orchestra pit. Currently, the multi-coloured Old Hill Street Police Station (formerly known as MICA Building) stands in its place.

But within a decade, the Assembly Rooms were falling into a dilapidated state, which is not surprising given that they had been constructed of lath, plaster and *attap* palm thatching. After their demolition in 1856, a temporary theatre was erected at the same spot. Performances continued there until 1861, primarily as fund-raisers for a theatre in the Town Hall under construction on Empress Place, which would later morph into Victoria Theatre.

1 The Old Hill Street Police Station, seen through the park's trees

2 1844 performance at Theatre Royal.

Drama Centre

A century later, a Cultural Centre was inaugurated on Canning Rise in 1955. Its name was changed to the Drama Centre in 1980. Mr. K.P. Bhaskar, founder of Bhaskar's Arts Academy was the first performer and went on to give lectures and demonstrations about Indian dance and art here.

While the building exterior appeared functional and bland, there was plenty of colour within, as many local performing arts companies used its 326-seat theatre, which presented landmark Singapore plays like *Lao Jiu, Army Daze and Mail Order Brides*.

This modest theatre was demolished in 2002 to make way for the glass-and-steel rear extension of the National Museum of Singapore. The Drama Centre now resides at the National Library in Victoria Street.

1 Announcement of a performance at the Drama Centre by Bhaskar's Academy of Dance.

2 The National Theatre.

National Theatre

Few young Singaporeans, and even fewer expats, know that until 1986, the park's slope at the corner of River Valley Road and Clemenceau Avenue was graced with the funky National Theatre. Opened on 8 August 1963 to commemorate Singapore's self-government, this 3,420-seat theatre, complete with revolving stage, was the venue for various international performances, universities' convocations and National Day Rallies.

Designed by acclaimed local architect Alfred Wong, its $2.2 million construction was financed in part by the public, through "a-dollar-a-brick" campaign with song requests over the radio. The southwestern slope of the hill had its shape changed with the addition of 16,500 ft3 of earth (taken from a former Teochew cemetery on Orchard Road), to accommodate the design of the theatre.

This unique building had a five-pointed façade (for the 5 stars on the flag) and a 150-tonne cantilevered steel roof stretching up the slopes of the hill – but no side or rear walls. People could opt to crash the show by sitting further up on the hill, behind the theatre, watching with binoculars or just listening. And understandably, some would ask Malay *bomohs* (shamans) to cast a "no rain" spell for a performance. Eventually, its days were ended due to structural problems with the cantilevered roof, wall-less structure, and noise pollution.

Performances and picnic baskets

With its location in the heart of the city, Fort Canning Hill attracts artists and event organisers who see it as the perfect venue for a range of performing arts and related cultural events.

Currently Fort Canning keeps a calendar full with a varied range of performances and shows that play to packed audiences. At these times the Fort Canning Green comes alive with thousands of people picnicking and watching the acts. The outdoor ambience in a tropical country like Singapore is enhanced by the park's green slope, the surrounding brick wall with gravestones set in and the view of the city.

Popular art performances at Fort Canning have resounded with audiences over the years.

Some of these became hugely popular with time, while many more are added as a part of the constantly evolving and vibrant art and music scene around Singapore.

above The park draws visitors for its many events such as a rock concert.

The Drama Festival

It was in 1984 when the green expanse at Fort Canning was used as a venue for an outdoor performance of the Drama Festival for the first time. The modern theatre performance was titled *The Sacred Marriage*, and boasted of a giant screen (that was previously unheard of) and interactive performances. The play was performed by National University of Singapore actors as well as by the performing group Talking Eyes. Details of the play were dramatically hushed before the performance.

By all accounts, the event was a huge success. Members of the public discussed the abstract performance for days afterwards. They were enthralled by the set-up and continuously debated the play's meaning. Finally a week later, *The Straits Times* ran an article written by the Director Bradley Winterton "lifting the shroud of mystery" surrounding *The Sacred Marriage* and offering an explanation to those who had been bewildered by the play.

It was an enthralling start to what would become a lively arts venue engaging the arts community and public at large.

Over the years, more performances followed and many more are added every year. Some are annual and some are perennial, but the line-up is constantly evolving. A few of these performances have particularly resounded with audiences over the years.

WOMAD

World of Music, Arts and Dance (WOMAD), an internationally renowned cultural festival, started playing in Singapore in 1998. It was one of the first big festivals to be held in Singapore, and continued to be a popular one for the next decade. It brought together artists from all over the globe celebrating the world's diversity of music, arts and dance in Fort Canning Hill.

Black Box performances

The 'black box' concept is a modern innovation of using a somewhat unadorned performance space to create a powerful dramatic impact. In Singapore, the audience has been treated to well-received plays by Theatreworks since the group moved in to Fort Canning Hill in the late 1980s.

Ballet under the Stars

A popular July event in the Singapore performing arts calendar, *Ballet under the Stars* is performed by the Singapore Dance Theatre. Started in the early 1990s, this is a family event where the audience can enjoy a picnic in the open as they watch a beautiful dance performance at Fort Canning Green. The event has almost come to be synonymous with performing arts at Fort Canning Hill.

Shakespeare in the Park

At Shakespeare in the Park, the audience is treated to one of the Bard's famous plays while they picnic on Fort Canning Green. The performance is organised and presented by the Singapore Repertory Theatre.

above Twelfth Night Poster.

A 'rocking' park

The open green expanse at Fort Canning is a wonderful setting for popular rock concerts. Well-known artists enjoy playing there, and since their music carries beyond the confines of the Green, others walking in the park enjoy listening as well! This venue continues to attract top musicians and performers and provides a unique concert atmosphere.

1 A truck belonging to a rock group that is about to set up their stage on Fort Canning Green – unloading in front of the Gothic Gates.

2 Rock the day away at Laneway Festival.

Tangible Art

Fort Canning Hill is the canvas of choice for exhibiting tangible art, as it provides such a perfect setting for creative expression.

In 1981, Singapore hosted the first ASEAN sculpture symposium, a project aimed at promoting a sense of community among member nations through visible symbols of tangible art created by sculptors from these countries. The entire symposium was documented on film as well by the Singapore Broadcasting Corporation, the predecessor of MediaCorp.

Art installations were donated by six member countries and are located throughout Fort Canning Hill. The sculptures are called *Unity* (from Indonesia), *Augury* (from Malaysia), *Fredesvinda* (from the Philippines), *Balance* (from Singapore), *Concentration* (from Thailand) and *Together* (from Brunei Darussalam).

1 "Spring of Life", a sculpture by Chua Boon Kee.

2 Welcoming a Chinese junk, designed by Eng Siak Loy, carved by Villa Frangipani.

With such a magnificent push, it was not long before the park became synonymous with creative public art installations that are integrated into the lush landscape of Fort Canning Hill.

Some art pieces are transitional or temporary installations and therefore lend a 'forever fresh' feel to the space. They are freely accessible and often stimulate interaction through touch or thought. They are beautiful visual treats!

1 ASEAN sculpture garden - Fredesvinda (1982), by Napoleon Veloso Abueva, The Philippines.

2 ASEAN sculpture garden - Unity (1982), by But Muchtar, Indonesia.

3 ASEAN sculpture garden - Balance (1982), by Ng Eng Teng, Singapore.

4 "Dance Dance Dance", an art installation by Chng Seok Tin and Aileen Toh.

5 Part of "Holy Audience", by P. Gnana.

Among other events that have taken place at Fort Canning was the International Wood Carving Symposium, with artists interpreting the theme "In Progress" and transforming fallen tree trunks into works of art. These artworks were placed at various venues around the hill.

Also, the Sculpture Society of Singapore often exhibits site-specific works at the Park.

Singapore artist Han Sai Por worked on sculptures made from trunks of tembusu trees as an artist-in-residence at Fort Canning Hill in 2009. She has also created a well-known sculpture titled Seeds (2006) consisting of two large kernels carved from sandstone excavated from Fort Canning Hill during the National Museum of Singapore's 2006 redevelopment.

Taking forward the theme of visual art, at the foot of the hill, where there used to be a swimming complex from 1959 to 2003, is now The Foothills Fort Canning Park, which includes a cosy cluster of art spaces. This conversion of the former swimming complex changing rooms and canteen into the Galeri Nila, Galeri Utama and Viridian Art House, provides a platform for artists to share their passion with art enthusiasts.

1 Legends of the Forbidden Hill, by Victor Tai Sheung Shing.

2 The Way to the Future, by Chow Shun Keung.

3 Together, by Osman Bin Mohammad, Brunei Darussalam.

4 "Seeds", by Han Sai Por.

Happenings

A lot happens in Fort Canning Hill!

1 The authors Jyoti and Melissa visiting the Battle Box.

2 Shopping is more enticing when located in the park.

3 A relaxing event at the park.

4 Looking down Coleman Street to Fort Canning Hill, early 19th century, by artist Chua Aik Boon. This is from National Parks Board's exhibition *A Landscape History of Singapore from Fort Canning Hill*.

1 A joyous place to stage community events (Orange Ribbon Celebrations/Racial Harmony Day).

2 A guide from National Parks Board leading an educational tour.

3 Practicing martial arts on a sunny morning.

4 In Her Shoes 2011 charity event.

5 Fitness training in the park.

4

An idyllic setting for celebrating a marriage after an official visit to the Registry of Marriages along Canning Rise

Impressions of the Hill

1 A school outing in the rain.

2 Off to a special occasion at the park.

3 Schoolchildren at Fort Canning Centre.

What does Fort Canning Hill mean to you?

"For me, the charm of Fort Canning is not an individual thing but the collective beauty of the park's environment. However, I have a real soft spot for the magnificent pair of sea eagles that were used to nesting in the communication tower. Unfortunately, the communication tower is no longer there but the familiar pitchy squawk of these beautiful birds is still commonplace. I have occasionally been treated to close-ups of the birds as they soar near to the ground in search of prey. Their wingspan is incredible, probably two metres across – they can block out the sun!"
By Darren Blakeley, founder of UFIT Urban Fitness

"Fort Canning is the perfect location . . . easy to get to by bus or train, a beautiful ambience and the layout of the park is ideal for performances. We hope to be able to stage Shakespeare in the Park there for many years to come."
By Charlotte Nors, Executive Director of the Singapore Repertory Theatre

In 1984, Gilles' group, The Talking Eyes, was involved in the first ever outdoor performance at Fort Canning Green in a very modern and abstract play. Gilles has some very fond memories of the park, especially in the evening when Fort Canning lent itself beautifully to the theme of the performance. The director used the various steps, slopes and other natural settings offered by the park green to create an impact for the almost 'ghost-like' characters of the play. He adds that Fort Canning, with its rich history and multifaceted personality is the heart and soul of Singapore.
From an interview with Gilles Massot, Singapore-based artist and Lecturer, Faculty of Fine Arts, LaSalle College of the Arts.

above "Government Hill from the New Harbour Road, Singapore 1844", by Charles Dyce.

"I used to arrive early at 9 am on Saturday mornings [for cub scout meetings] before everyone else. I was curious enough to wonder who were buried beside these tombstones that dotted around the cemetery and strange as they seemed, these are large grave stones and there was one in particular that was located right in the middle of the field. It measured something like 3 ft x 6 ft and 3 ft high. I have never noticed the inscription on it . . . we simply used it as our convenient table to land our personal bags. I sometimes wondered who was buried right beneath the slabs. We were asked to come in dressed in our cub uniform, I remember."
From "Fort Canning", by Simon Chu, February 13, 2006 entry in http://goodmorningyesterday.blogspot.com

"Just then I saw a terap tree and thought I would take a short rest. I sat on the cool ground with my back against the large trunk of the tree and promptly dozed off to the cacophony of nature. Suddenly I heard the most melodious voice humming a tune. It was most soothing and wonderful. I turned and craned my neck, and saw a beautiful lady on the other side of the terap tree. She was picking the fallen terap bark, presumably to use as basket linings, and oblivious to all around her. . .

Then, I shared that the best part for me about Bukit Larangan was the natural beauty of the flora and fauna. To my surprise, she said "You too? I thought I was the only one. . . ." Then, I knew that I had found my soul mate . . ." [sic]
An excerpt from *Ah Gong's Diary* (http://fortcanningancient.blogspot.com). Seven young people were inspired to write a blog recounting their trips to Fort Canning Hill to retrace the steps that their grandfather had recorded in his diary. This entry recounts how their grandfather met his future wife.

For this Aikido teacher who chooses to give early morning classes near Fort Gate, the park provides two things. One, a connection between the martial art of aikido and the martial history of the park so evident in the surrounding fort wall and Sally Port. Two, a communion with the magnificent trees.
Thierry Diagana, 4th Dan instructor at Mumei Shudan Dojo

[The hill] was for a time the stomping ground of Anglo-Chinese Primary School pupils. We only had to step out of the school compound to find ourselves in the world of Fort Canning. I have fond memories of playing football on the grassy slopes, collecting insects and seeds, and wandering among the gravestones. Fort Canning was a wild place then, holding in store many wonders for an eleven-year-old to discover.

But Bukit Larangan has not yielded all its secrets; a touch of magic from the old world lingers. And if you listen carefully on a quiet evening, you may even hear the spirits of kings and governors tell their stories in the whispers of the leaves and stones.
Terry Ho, author of *The Forbidden Hill Chronicles*, an epic fantasy series inspired by Fort Canning Hill.

66 If I were to dig this spot I'm standing on right here in the Fort Canning Centre car park, I dare say I'll find something," he says. "Any piece of land or step or area you stand on could house an amazing artefact. My reality is digging out the past, trying to find out who I am, where I came from, where I'm going, why I belong here. These are inherent questions an archaeologist would ponder. And that's why I dig – I am seeking these answers. 99

Mr. Lim Chen Sian, well-known Singaporean archaeologist from the National University of Singapore Southeast Asian Studies Programme. This quote is from an article available at http://www.singaporekopitiam.sg/places-and-heritage/places/historical-landmarks

opposite page Having lunch at the picnic terrace.

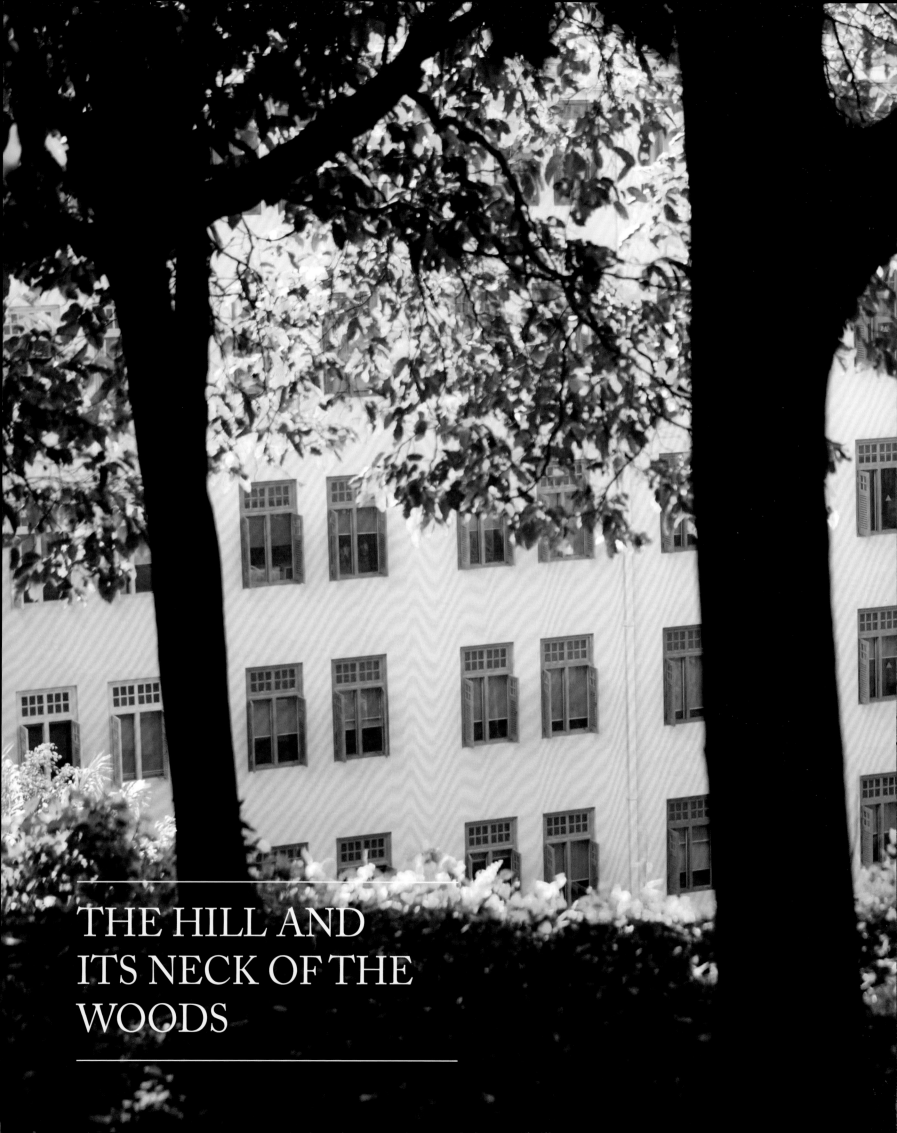

THE HILL AND
ITS NECK OF THE
WOODS

Overview

Fort Canning Hill forms a vibrant and integral part of its neighbourhood.

In the first half of the 19th century, the hill was surrounded by nutmeg and clove plantations to the west (around Oxley Road) and the north (around Prinsep Street). Many of the wealthy European and Chinese proprietors built homes along Orchard Road and River Valley Road, bordering the hill.

Within the area once covered by the Botanic & Experimental Garden, schools, libraries, museums, and places of worship have been erected over the years to serve the population. The first of these was a church, dating from 1835. The concentration of museums in the neighborhood contributed to it becoming an anchor for the Museum Planning Area. Many of the buildings are still standing - some used for their original purposes, and some not.

1 Fort Canning Hill and its neighbourhood: as depicted in CUBE (Challenge for the Urban and Built Environment 2011), an annual student workshop organised by the Urban Redevelopment Authority (URA).

2 View of the park, from River Valley Road.

Museums

Fort Canning Hill sits within the Museum Planning Area, which, as its name suggests, houses numerous museums. Though Singapore is home to more than 50 fascinating museums and heritage galleries, it has not always appreciated art the way it does today. A 1949 (anonymous) article in *The Straits Times* had this to say:

"The number of people in Singapore today who would appreciate an art gallery is very small. . . . Such facilities never having existed in Singapore, the vast majority of people are unable to tell a good picture from a bad one. But even a small art gallery would be a beginning in the process of teaching the people of this city to look at life through the eyes of the artist."

How things have changed since those artless, post-war years!

National Museum of Singapore

Opened in 1887 as the Raffles Museum and Library, the National Museum of Singapore is Singapore's oldest museum. The original museum was known for its collections of Southeast Asian natural history, ethnology, and archeology. Today's progressive museum focuses on Singapore's history and dynamic culture, along with featuring exhibits of international collections.

In 2006, the elegant neo-classical museum reopened after extensive renovation, and the addition of a modern glass-and-steel extension. As stated in a panel in front of the museum, the stately, original Rotunda Dome of the museum apparently was so difficult to construct that it drove its first contractor to madness! The new Glass Rotunda, which is the entry to the History Gallery, was designed as a modern interpretation of the old Rotunda.

1 History of the venerable National Museum of Singapore.

2 *Pedas Pedas* (Chilli), by Kumari Nahappan.

Singapore Philatelic Museum

above The Singapore Philatelic Museum today

The Singapore Philatelic Museum, the first of its kind in Southeast Asia, contains collections of stamps and archival philatelic material of Singapore from the 1830s, such as stamps from member countries of the Universal Postal Union. It is housed in a charming building from 1906, at the northeastern edge of the park.

The first Anglo-Chinese School moved from Amoy Street to Canning Rise in 1887. In 1906, an extension of the school was built down the street. After the school moved out, the building was occupied for a while by the Methodist Book Room, before the Singapore Philatelic Museum moved here in 1995.

Peranakan Museum

Merchants from abroad have always been attracted to the trading hubs of Southeast Asia (e.g., Singapore, Melaka, Penang, Batavia). Many chose to settle in their new communities, and marry local women. The Malay term "peranakan" means "locally born", and refers to the hybrid populations and cultures that resulted: Peranakan Chinese (Chinese), Chitty Melaka (South Indian Hindu), Jawi Peranakans (South Indian Muslim), and Eurasian Peranakans (Dutch, Portuguese).

The Peranakan Museum showcases the cultures of these Peranakan communities in a building designed in an "Eclectic Classical" style: a fusion of classical, tropical, and colonial styles. The museum occupies the former home of the Tao Nan School, completed in 1912. The building was renovated and opened as the Asian Civilisations Museum in 1997. In 1998, it was gazetted as a national monument and became home to the Peranakan Museum in 2008.

Religious Buildings

A combination of the hill's central location with the peaceful atmosphere it inspires have undoubtedly encouraged people to build their places of worship nearby. Scattered around the park's perimeter are several Christian churches, a Hindu temple, and a Jewish synagogue.

Armenian Apostolic Church of St. Gregory the Illuminator

SINGAPORE.

VIEW OF GOVERNMENT HILL, THE ENGLISH BURIAL GROUND AND THE ARMENIAN CHURCH.

London Pub. Feb. 1840, by Ackermann & Co.

above An 1840 view of the hill, showing the Armenian Church at its base, by artist C.H. Smith and engraver G.S. Madeley

The original Botanical and Experimental Garden was discontinued in 1829, and some of their land was sold to the Armenian community to build a church. The Armenian Church was not only the first Christian church to have been built on the island (1835), but it was also designed and built by George Coleman, Singapore's pioneering colonial architect. The majestic church was gazetted as a national monument in 1973.

The most famous tombstone in the church's graveyard is that of Miss Agnes Joaquim,

the daughter of an Armenian merchant and philanthropist. An avid gardener and orchid breeder, she won first prize at an 1899 flower show for her hybrid, Vanda Miss Joaquim, which was proclaimed Singapore's national flower in 1981.

When the Christian Cemetery on Fort Canning Green was closed in the mid-1950s, several tombstones and statues were moved to the garden of this church. Miss Joaquim's tomb, however, was moved here from the Bukit Timah Cemetery.

Sri Thendayuthapani temple

Hindus have been worshipping on the site of the Sri Thendayuthapani Temple even before there was a temple. The early Nattukkottai Chettiars initially offered their prayers under a pipal tree (*Ficus religiosa*), beside a tank filled from a waterfall on the side of Fort Canning Hill. In 1859, they were able to construct the first temple in honor of Sri Thendayuthapani, or Lord Muruga. They bought the land from the nutmeg estate of Charles Oxley (whose name today graces a nearby road).

The temple, along with its impressive gopuram, was rebuilt in 1983. During the Thaipusam holiday, devotees walk from the Sri Srinivasa Perumal Temple along Serangoon Road, all the way to this temple, the "Chettiars' Temple".

Cathedral of the Good Shepherd

Built in the 1840s, the Cathedral of the Good Shepherd is the oldest Catholic church in Singapore. Originally a church, it was elevated to cathedral status in 1888, and was gazetted as a national monument in 1973.

In 1832, an earlier, rickety church had been built on land granted to the church by Raffles. When that building needed to be expanded and replaced, Parish Priest Father Jean-Marie Beurel preferred to keep the site for a Catholic school - St. Joseph's Institution (now the Singapore Art Museum) was eventually built there in 1867. The new Renaissance style church was built on adjacent Queen Street, on land granted to the church by Governor Bonham.

Orchard Road Presbyterian Church

The Orchard Road Presbyterian Church was the earliest Presbyterian church in Singapore. It was founded by the Scottish community and built in 1878.

1 The gopuram and a resident rooster.

2 Cathedral of the Good Shepherd.

Chesed-El Synagogue

Chesed-El Synagogue, the second synagogue to be built in Singapore, was established in 1905. Designed in the Palladian style, it was gazetted as a national monument in 1998. Manassah Meyer, a wealthy Jewish trader and real estate tycoon, had it built as his private synagogue, on his estate on Oxley Rise.

Wesley Methodist Church

The building of the Wesley Methodist Church, the "mother church" of Methodism in the region, dates from 1909. It was initiated by William Oldham, the first Bishop of the Methodist church in Malaya. The earlier church held services at the Town Hall, until the governor granted it 3530m² along Fort Canning Hill in 1907.

Church of the Sacred Heart

This church was built by the Society of Saint Vincent de Paul in 1910, with funding from three wealthy Chinese benefactors. It primarily serves the Cantonese and Hakka community.

Located on Tank Road, for its first 30 years the church was neighbours with the Tank Road railway station, and it looked out upon the railway. Today, in memory of those times, one of the church's buildings bears the sign "Tank Station".

above Chesed-El Synagogue.

Learning Institutions

Fort Canning Hill and its immediate surroundings was home to numerous schools and libraries for over a century.

St. Andrew's School

St. Andrew's School, affiliated with the Anglican Church, was founded in 1861 as the St. Andrew's Church of England Mission School. In 1875, it moved to a 1.6 ha piece of land on the then Government Hill along Stamford Road. Its alumni include David Marshall (1st Chief Minister of Singapore) and Benjamin Sheares (2nd President of Singapore).

By the 1930s, the site became too cramped, and importantly, lacked a playing field for the school's star rugby team, prompting the school to move to Woodsville (Potong Pasir). The Fort Canning site was demolished in 1953, and the National Library was built in its place in 1960.

Anglo-Chinese Primary School

Anglo-Chinese School, Singapore.

The Methodist Church and Canning Rise have a long history together. In 1886, Bishop William Oldham, the first Bishop of the Methodist church in Malaya, founded the Methodist Episcopal chapel on the site of today's National Archives. That same year, Bishop Oldham set up the Anglo-Chinese School on Amoy Street. In 1887, the school moved to a new building on Canning Rise next to the chapel, where it remained for over 100 years. By 1906, more room was needed, and down the street, an extension was built, which today houses the Singapore Philatelic Museum.

Raffles Girls' School

Established in the mid-19th century, Raffles Girls' School moved to the corner of Queen Street and Stamford Road in 1928. It remained there until its 1959 move to Anderson Road, where it continues with its mission to nurture "Daughters of a Better Age".

1 1890 view of the Anglo-Chinese School.

2 Original school fence of Raffles Girls' School.

3 The National Library building, by artist Buz Walker.

4 Plaque from the former United Chinese Library.

LAST DAYS of NATIONAL LIBRARY
28 MARCH 04   ABOUT 2½ HOURS

Teochew Building

The Ngee Ann Kongsi is based in the imposing Teochew Building on Tank Road, dating from the early 1960s. The Kongsi is involved in educational, cultural, and welfare activities. The building formerly housed Tuan Mong High School, which replaced the earlier Tuan Mong School established there in 1906. Ngee Ann College, the predecessor of Ngee Ann Polytechnic, opened there in 1963.

United Chinese Library

Dr. Sun Yat Sen, the Father of Modern China, inaugurated this library in 1910 at its original location just below Fort Canning Hill. The following year it was moved to nearby Armenian Street, where it remained until a 1987 move to Cantonment Road.

The library was originally set up to spread general knowledge among Singaporeans. It then became a centre promoting the cause of the Chinese Revolution, and later supporting anti-Japanese activities during the 1930s when China was under Japanese attack.

National Library

There has been a library in Singapore since the Singapore Institution began collecting the literature of the region in 1823. In 1874, the library was incorporated into the new Raffles Library and Museum.

The library, however, had always been a "proprietary" library, and was not free. By the 1950s, the public was clamoring for a free, public library. Lee Kong Chian, a multimillionaire rubber magnate, made a large donation to build the new National Library of Singapore on the site of the chapel of the former St. Andrew's school.

Moving day came in 1960. Forty library staff formed a human chain from the old to new buildings to move 150,000 books. The new library contained copies of all publications printed in the colony. It held story-telling sessions for children to inspire reading among them. It organised a Mobile Library Service to bring some of its books out into the larger community. And significantly, it had collections of books not only in English but also in the vernacular languages.

For generations of Singaporeans, going to the library was a Saturday outing. Reading, relaxing, meeting friends, and having *roti prata* and *sarabat* (milk tea) at the stalls next to the carpark were all ways to spend an afternoon. Students would also come to study from nearby schools, such as Raffles Girls' School, St Joseph's Institution (today's Singapore Art Museum) and Tao Nan School (today's Peranakan Museum).

The 1992 Civic District Master Plan decreed that the future Fort Canning Tunnel would run beneath the library, which would have to go. When Singaporeans learned of this, many opposed the plan. The library had been so important - intellectually and emotionally - to so many over the years that no one wanted to see it disappear. In 2004, the collections were moved to the new Victoria Street location. The current National Library building on Victoria Street contains not only the books from the Stamford library, but also a commemorative wall built from 5,000 of its red bricks.

Fort

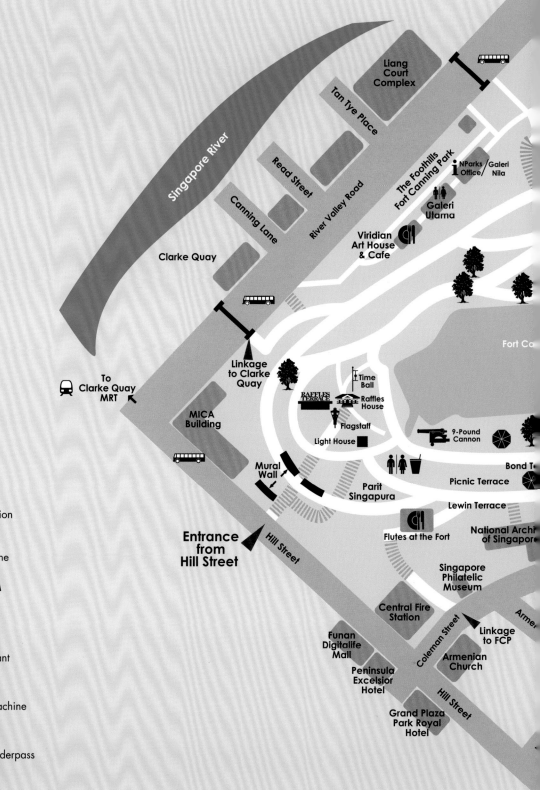

Singapore River

Liang Court Complex

Tan Tye Place

Read Street

Canning Lane

River Valley Road

The Foothills Fort Canning Park

NParks / Galeri Office / Nila

Galeri Utama

Viridian Art House & Cafe

Clarke Quay

To Clarke Quay MRT

Linkage to Clarke Quay

Time Ball

RAFFLES TERRACE

Raffles House

MICA Building

Flagstaff

Light House

9-Pound Cannon

Fort Ca

Bond T

Mural Wall

Parit Singapura

Picnic Terrace

Lewin Terrace

Entrance from Hill Street

Hill Street

Flutes at the Fort

National Archi of Singapore

Singapore Philatelic Museum

Central Fire Station

Coleman Street

Linkage to FCP

Armer

Funan Digitalife Mall

Armenian Church

Peninsula Excelsior Hotel

Hill Street

Grand Plaza Park Royal Hotel

Legend

Tarmac Road

Track

Ancient History Walking Trail

Trees of the Fort Walking Trail

Colonial History Walking Trail

Staircase/Steps

Escalator

Building

Carpark

Old Cemetery Wall

i
Information

☎
Telephone

Toilet

Restaurant

Vending Machine

P
Pedestrian Underpass

Shelter

Heritage Tree

MRT Station

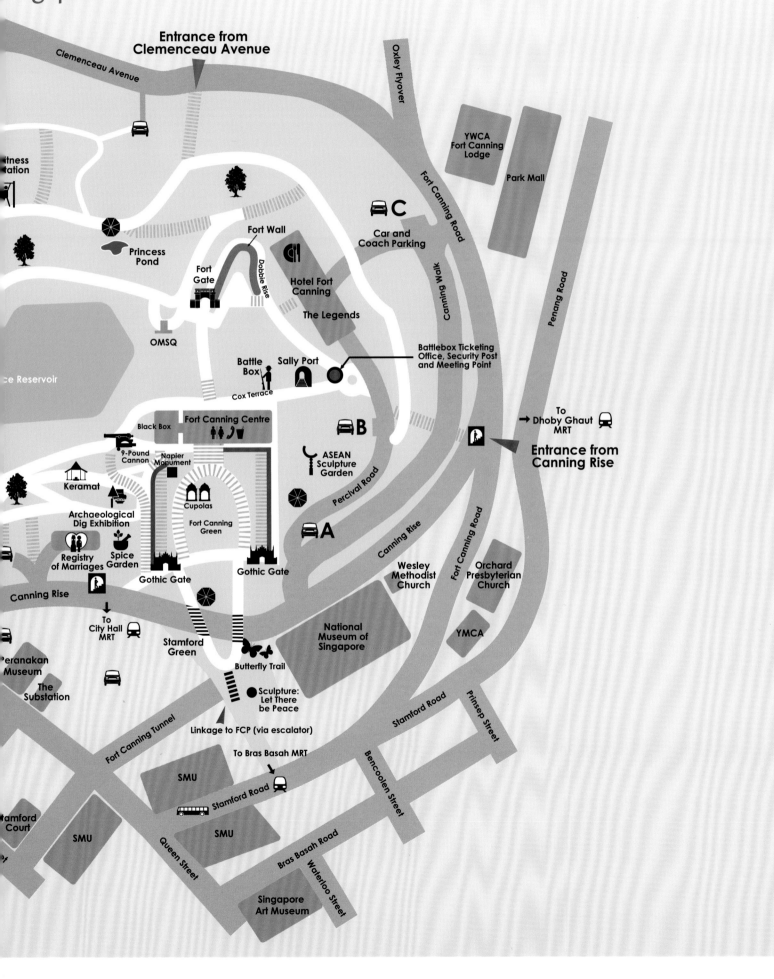

anning Park
Singapore

Entrance from Clemenceau Avenue

Clemenceau Avenue

Oxley Flyover

YWCA Fort Canning Lodge

Park Mall

Fort Canning Road

itness tation

Princess Pond

Fort Wall

C
Car and Coach Parking

Canning Walk

Penang Road

Fort Gate

Dobbie Rise

Hotel Fort Canning

The Legends

OMSQ

Battlebox Ticketing Office, Security Post and Meeting Point

Battle Box

Sally Port

e Reservoir

Cox Terrace

To Dhoby Ghaut MRT

Entrance from Canning Rise

B

Black Box

Fort Canning Centre

ASEAN Sculpture Garden

Percival Road

9-Pound Cannon

Napier Monument

Keramat

Cupolas

Canning Rise

Archaeological Dig Exhibition

Fort Canning Green

A

Registry of Marriages

Spice Garden

Gothic Gate

Gothic Gate

Wesley Methodist Church

Fort Canning Road

Orchard Presbyterian Church

Canning Rise

To City Hall MRT

Stamford Green

YMCA

Peranakan Museum

The Substation

Butterfly Trail

National Museum of Singapore

Sculpture: Let There be Peace

Stamford Road

Prinsep Street

Fort Canning Tunnel

Linkage to FCP (via escalator)

To Bras Basah MRT

Bencoolen Street

tamford Court

SMU

Stamford Road

SMU

SMU

Queen Street

Bras Basah Road

Waterloo Street

Singapore Art Museum

AUTHORS' ACKNOWLEDGEMENTS

How could we NOT have written a book about Fort Canning Hill?

Daily walks with the dog, weekend breakfasts at the Picnic Terrace, evenings lying on the Green listening to concerts – the hill has become such a special part of our lives. Through this book, we hope to bring to light what made Fort Canning Hill so special to us. Whether you are visiting Singapore, or whether you live here, we want to show you why Fort Canning has a reason to be a part of your life too.

Of course for any book to materialise, the idea needs someone to believe in it. Some of our earliest support and guidance came from Professor Tommy Koh, for which we are extremely grateful.

Professor John Miksic's groundbreaking research in uncovering ancient Singapore played an integral role in motivating us, and his generous input has been invaluable.

We would like to thank everyone who helped us in this adventure, starting of course with our patiently supportive and encouraging families. We are also indebted to the staff at National Parks Board, Brett Gold, Gilles Massot, K.P. Bhaskar, Grant Pereira, and the wonderful Urban Sketchers who have added so much colour to our book.

There have been many more people who went out of their way to respond to our requests for information, photographs, and images. We would like to let you know that we truly appreciate your efforts and generosity.

Several organisations have been very forthcoming about sharing their rich collections: the National Archives of Singapore, the National Museum of Singapore, the National Parks Board, the Peranakan Museum, the Urban Redevelopment Authority, the Land Transport Authority, and the National Library.

We would also like to thank ORO Editions team – Gordon Goff for his willingness to take on this book, Melanie Lee for her support and logistics, See Chee Keong for his magic with the camera, and D Tjandra for design and layout.

Last but certainly not least, this book would never have existed without the enthusiasm of the National Heritage Board and the backing from their Heritage Industry Incentive Program (HI²P). The HI²P encourages those like ourselves who desire to showcase Singapore's rich and varied heritage.

ABOUT THE AUTHORS

Jyoti Angresh   Melissa Diagana

Jyoti Angresh and Melissa Diagana are two expatriates who have been living in Singapore for over six years. Having lived near Fort Canning Hill, they were constantly amazed by this multifaceted and centrally-located park. They were inspired to write this book to share their enthusiasm for this hidden jewel, and to highlight the impressive history and ecology contained within the hill.

Jyoti is a qualified fashion business professional, with a degree in the humanities. She has a natural love for heritage and culture that has found expression in her writings over the years.

Melissa is a molecular biologist by training, who enjoys studying the broader picture of natural history as much as its reductionist details. She regularly writes about nature and environmental topics.

REFERENCES

We have used innumerable resources while writing this book. Below is a selection that should be the most useful to readers interested in delving into a subject in more detail.

Books

Acton, Grace
"Herbes to season, herbes to cure"
Reference MS.1, 1621
Wellcome Library cookbook collection
(http://library.wellcome.ac.uk/node9300909.
html > recipe manuscripts online)

Baker, Nick and Lim, Kelvin K.P. (co-ordinators)
Wild Animals of Singapore
Draco Publishing, 180 pp, 2008

Bastin, John and Kwa, Chong Guan
Natural History Drawings: The Complete William Farquhar Collection, Malay Penninsula 180-3-1818.
Editions Didier Millet, 335 pp, 2010

Buckley, Charles Burton
Around Fort Canning Hill in the 19th Century: An anecdotal history of old times in Singapore, from the Foundation of the Settlement on February 6th, 1819, To the Transfer to the Colonial Office as part of the Colonial Possessions of the Crown on April 1st, 1867.
Fraser & Neave, 1902; now Oxford University Press, 1984

Joly, Eric, Larpin, Denis, and De Franceschi, D.
Les grandes serres du Jardin des Plantes
Editions du Pommier / Les Editions de Musée, 191 pp, 2010

Miksic, John N. and Low, Cheryl-Ann M.G.
Early Singapore, 1300s-1819: Evidence in maps, text and artefacts
Singapore History Museum, 148 pp, 2004

Ng, Angie B.C, et al.
A Guide to the Fabulous Figs of Singapore
Singapore Science Centre, 152 pp, 2005

Simmonds, Peter Lund
The commercial products of the vegetable kingdom, considered in their various uses to man and in their relation to the arts and manufactures; Forming a practical treatise & handbook of reference for the colonist, manufacturer, merchant, and consumer, on the cultivation, preparation for shipment, and commercial value, &c of the various substances obtained from trees and plants, entering into the husbandry of tropical and sub-tropical regions, &c.
T.F.A. Day publishers, 1854

Sodhi, Navjot S. and Ehrlich, Paul R. (editors)
Conservation Biology for All.
Oxford University Press, Oxford, 344 pp., 2010

Tan, Hugh T.W, Chou, L.M., Yeo, Darren C.J., and Ng, Peter K.L.
The Natural Heritage of Singapore
Prentice Hall, 271 pp, 2007, 2nd ed.

Tee Swee Ping (editor)
Trees of our garden city.
National Parks Board, 382 pp, 2009, 2nd ed.

Wallace, Alfred R.
The Malay Archipelago: The Land of the Orang-utan and the Bird of Paradise.
Periplus Editions, 488 pp, 2008

Websites

Sites with information on multiple subjects:

• Ecology Asia, www.ecologyasia.com

• Flora Fauna Web,
  http://florafaunaweb.nparks.gov.sg

• Ministry of Defence, Singapore,
  www.mindef.gov.sg

• National Archives of Singapore,
  www.a2o.com.sg

• National Parks Board, Singapore,
  www.nparks.gov.sg

• Raffles Museum of Biodiversity Research natural history news,
  http://habitatnews.nus.edu.sg

- Singapore Heritage Trails, http://heritagetrails.sg
- Singapore Infopedia, http://infopedia.nl.sg
- Singapore newspaper archive, http://newspapers.nl.sg
- Urban Redevelopment Authority, www.ura.gov.sg
- Wikipedia, http://en.wikipedia.org
- Wild Singapore, www.wildsingapore.com

More specific sites:
- Anglo-Chinese School, www.acs.sch.edu.sg
- Armenian Church, http://armeniansinasia.org
- Flutes at the Fort restaurant, www.flutes.com.sg
- Hotel Fort Canning, www.hfcsingapore.com
- National Museum of Singapore, www.nationalmuseum.sg
- Ngee Ann Polytechnic, www.np.edu.sg
- Orchard Road Presbyterian Church, www.orpc.sg
- Peranakan Museum, www.peranakanmuseum.sg
- Singapore Philatelic Museum, www.spm.org.sg
- Sports Museum, www.sportsmuseum.com.sg

- Sri Thendayuthapani Temple, www.sttemple.com
- Wesley Methodist Church, www.wesleymc.org
- YMCA, www.ymca.org.sg

Blogs:
- http://fortcanningancient.blogspot.sg
- http://goodmorningyesterday.blogspot.com
- http://siewkumhong.blogspot.com
- http://thelongnwindingroad.wordpress.com

Personal communication

- "I want to remember... the old performing spaces" exhibit at the Singapore Arts Festival 2011
- Trees of the Fort walk, 12 Feb 2011 with Grant Pereira of The Green Volunteers
- Fort Canning Revisited, 27 July 2011 NParks tour
- Interview with Mr. Bhaskar, 12 Jan 2012
- Original Singapore Walks, 14 Jan 2012
- Interview with Prof. Gilles Massot, 21 Feb 2012
- Prof. Johannes Widodo NUS walking tour 21 April 2012

1 Plain Tiger butterfly, on snakeweed.

CREDITS

Many people supplied images, information and content that helped to make this book as rich as it is. For these contributions, we would like to thank:

Amar-Singh HSS

Benedick Lim

Buz Walker

Charlotte Nors

Choo Meng Foo

Clara Wong

Cyril Wong

Darren Blakeley

Dhruv Angresh

e'von le angelis

Han Sai Por

Jason Tay

Kit Madula

Kumari Nahappan

Lat

Nanthinee Jeevanandam

Nick Baker

Pocholo Estremos

Rachel Mok

Rey Villegas

Terry Ho

The Fig and the Wasp blog

Thierry Diagana

Tia Boon Sim

Zaihan Kariyani

PHOTOGRAPHY CREDITS

See Chee Keong
Pages: 2, 3 , 4-5, 7, 8, 10, 12, 17, 18, 20 (image 1), 27, 30 (image 1), 35, 37 (image 3), 40 (image 1, 2), 40 (image 4), 45 (image 3), 48-49, 50 (image 1), 51, 53, 60, 70-71, 76-77, 78, 79 (image 1), 83, 84-85, 87 (image 3), 89, 93, 94 (image 2), 95, 100-101, 104 (image 1), 106, 112, 114 (images 1-3), 115, 116 (image 2), 121, 122-123, 124 (image 2, 3), 126, 128-129, 131, 132 (image 1, 2), 133, 134-135, 136, 140 (image 2), 144, 151, 152-153

Melissa Diagana
Pages: 14 (image 1), 15, 21, 23, 34 (image 1), 36 (image 1), 41 (image 6), 57, 63 (image 3), 64, 66 (image 2), 67, 69 (image 5), 72 (image 1), 73 (image 3, 5, 7), 74 (image 2), 80 (image 1, 2), 82, 87 (image 1, 2), 88, 90 (image 1, 3), 91 (image 4), 92 (image 1), 94 (image 1), 98 (images 1-3), 99 (image 4, 7), 103, 111 (image 1), 113, 114 (image 4), 116 (image 1), 117 (image 3), 119, 120 (image 3), 124 (image 1), 138 (image 1), 141 (image 4)

Amar-Singh HSS
Page: 14 (image 2)

Magma Studios Pte Ltd
Pages: 14 (image 3), 34 (image 2)

National Parks Board
Pages: 16 (image 1), 22 (image 1, 3), Pages: 24 (image 2), 32 (image 2), 34 (image 3), 42 (image 2), 44 (image 1), 61 (image 2), 66 (image 3), 68, 72 (image 2), 73 (image 4, 6), 79 (image 2), 81 (images 3-5), 86 (image 1), 96 (images 1-3), 97 (image 4, 5), 111 (image 2), 120 (image 2), 142-143, 147 (image 1)

National Museum of Singapore, National Heritage Board
Pages: 16 (image 2, 3), 22 (image 2), 24 (image 1), 25 (image 2), 31, 38 (image 3), 55 (image 4), 66 (image 1, 4), 125, 137

National Archives of Singapore, MICA Collection
Pages: 19, 37 (image 2)

Wikimedia Commons
Pages: 22 (image 4), 26 (image 1), 33

National Archives of Singapore
Pages: 26 (image 2), 32 (image 1), 34, 40 (image 3), 43, 54 (image 1, 2), 56, 58, 59 (image 2), 61 (image 1), 62, 102, 140 (image 1)

Singapore Tourist Promotion Board
Page: 43

Flutes at the Fort
Page: 45 (image 2)

Hotel Fort Canning Singapore
Pages: 46 (image 2), 55 (image 3)

Professor John Miksic
Page: 52 (image 1, 2)

Singapore Land Authority
Pages: 54 (image 2), 59 (image 2)

Land Transport Authority
Page: 59 (image 3)

Jyoti Angresh
Pages: 69 (images 1-4), 109, 118 (image 2, 3)

Kumari Nahappan
Page: 74 (image 1)

Choo Meng Foo
Page 22 (image 1), 42 (image 2), 44 (image 1), 80 (image 3)

Nanthinee Jeevanandam
Page: 86 (image 2)

The Fig & The Wasp (www.thefigandthewasp.com)
Page: 86 (image 3)

National Museum of Singapore, National Heritage Board, Gift of Mr G.K. Goh
Pages: 90 (image 2), 09 (image 5)

Peranakan Museum, Singapore
Page: 92 (images 2-4)

Thierry Diagana
Page: 99 (image 5)

Nick Baker, EcologyAsia.com
Page: 99 (image 6)

Lim Kheng Chye's Collection, National Archives of Singapore
Page: 26 (image 2), 104 (image 2), 105 (image 3)

Scott Henderson
Page: 105

National Library Board
Page: 107

Bhaskar's Academy of Dance
Page: 108 (image 1)

National Arts Council and Living Portraits
Page: 108 (image 2)

Singapore Repertory Theatre
Page: 110

Jack Lee. Creative Commons Attribution ShareAlike 3.0 licence (http://creativecommons.org/licenses/by-sa/3.0), via the Wikimedia Commons.
Page: 117 (image 4)

Central Singapore Community Development Council
Page: 120 (image 1)

Simon Wong and Chemistry Singapore
Page: 120 (image 4)

Melissa Diagana and Urban Redevelopment Authority
Page: 130

Singapore Philatelic Museum
Page: 133

Preservation of Monuments Board
Pages: 138 (image 2), 139

Singapore City Gallery, Urban Redevelopment Authority
Front endpaper

UNION J

A 2014 ANNUAL

Written by Sarah Milne
Designed by Jane Greig

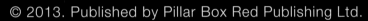

PBR

A Pillar Box Red Publication

© 2013. Published by Pillar Box Red Publishing Ltd.

ISBN: 978-1-907823-51-0

CON·TENTS

THE STORY

GEORGE SHELLEY

Joshua Thomas John "Josh" Cuthbert was born on 28 July 1992 in Ascot. Before becoming a member of Union J, Josh had worked in IT sales, and also played football at a high standard.

Josh had been approached Jayne Collins, the former manager of 'The Wanted' to join the band, but could not accept as he was still In a two-year contract that he signed with his formerband, 'Replay'.
Josh and Jaymi first met at Sylvia Young Theatre School and were then introduced them to JJ creating Triple J - what the band were called before becoming Union J.

George Paul Shelley was born on 27 July 1993 in Clevedon. Before becoming a member of Union J, George was a graphic design student, working part-time in a local coffee shop.

George came to the X Factor auditions as a solo artist. He sang 'Toxic' by Britney Spears, got through to bootcamp, but thought his journey had finished there. This later turned out not to be the case.
He got his first guitar at the age of 13 and with the help of his granddad, taught himself to play. Even when he was just a toddler, he was always keen to be part of family get-togethers, getting mum Toni to fill up bottles with rice to use as a maraca so he could make music.

JOSH CUTHBERT

SO FAR

JJ HAMBLETT

James William "Jaymi" Hensley was born on 24 February 1990 in Luton. Jaymi met Josh at Sylvia Young Theatre School and was one of the original members of Triple J.

Before being in the band, Jaymi was a teaching assistant, teaching music and drama. Jaymi came out as gay to his family when he was about 14 and to the nation during the X Factor live finals - he has a steady boyfriend, Olly.

JAYMI HENSLEY

Jamie Paul "JJ" Hamblett was born on 25 May 1988 in Newmarket. He changed his name to JJ to avoid potential confusion with bandmate Jaymi Hensley.

As well as an actor and a model, JJ used to be a jockey, racing horses - in fact he once even rode in a race for the Queen. Unfortunately his height and weight meant that he would never be able to make a living out of being a jockey (they are famously very short and very thin). This was a very disappointing time for him, as being a jockey had been his childhood dream.
Luckily for JJ, he then got the opportunity to form Triple J with Josh and Jaymi, and he says that this was the luckiest break for him at just the right time.

JOSH FACTFILE

NAME Joshua Thomas John Cuthbert

BIRTHDATE 28 July 1992 **STARSIGN** Leo

HEIGHT 5'11 **HOMETOWN** Ascot

FAMILY Mum and Dad, Kathryn and Graham. Josh also has a brother called Callum and a sister called Victoria

BEFORE UNION J Josh worked in IT sales!

CELEBRITY CRUSH Louis Walsh???

KNOWN AS The 'funny one' in Union J, also the loudest and most romantic

LIKES Sunglasses and Deal or No Deal

RANDOM FACTS He can sing 'Hero' in Spanish, his favourite cartoon character is Shrek

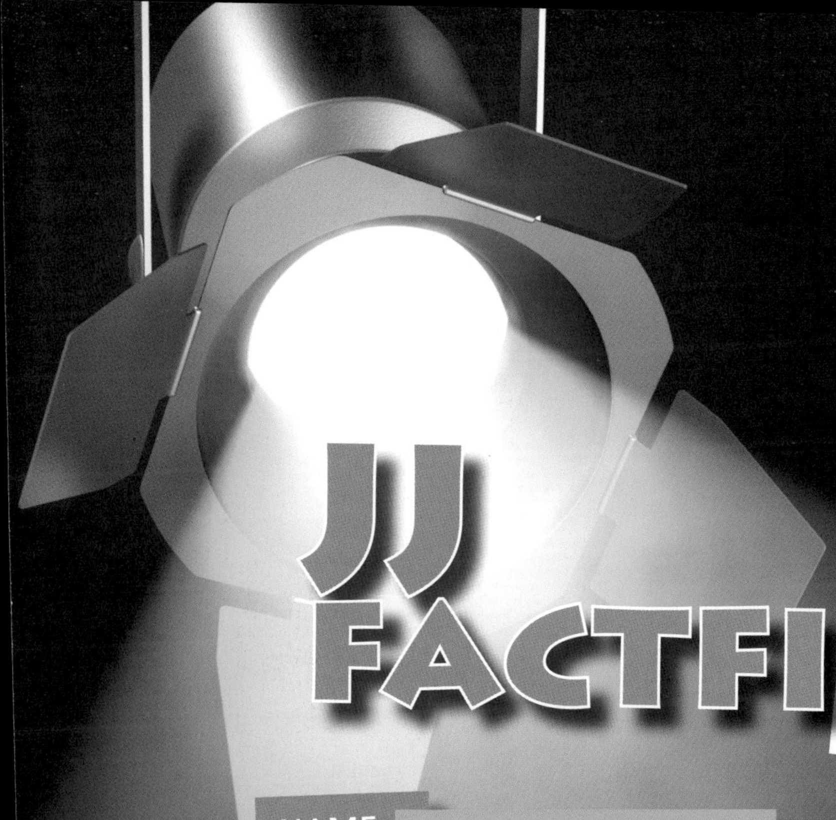

JJ FACTFILE

NAME Jamie Paul Hamblett

BIRTHDATE 25 May 1988

STARSIGN Gemini

HEIGHT 5' 10

HOMETOWN Newmarket

FAMILY A brother called Ashley and a sister called Otea

BEFORE UNION J JJ was a jockey, a model and actor

CELEBRITY CRUSH Michelle Keegan from Corrie

KNOWN AS 'Dopey Spice' by the other boys, for being a bit slower than everyone else!

LIKES Tattoos and giraffes

RANDOM FACTS He changed his name to JJ to avoid confusion between him and Jaymi, if he could be a vegetable he would be a sprout

we love you...

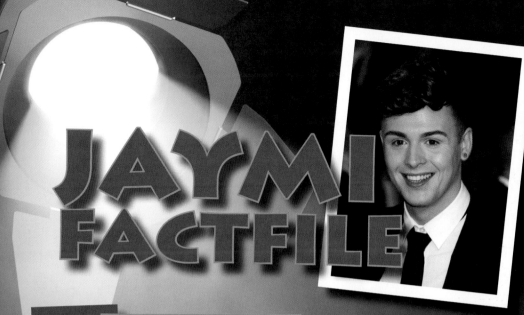

JAYMI FACTFILE

NAME James William Hensley

BIRTHDATE 24 February 1990

STARSIGN Pisces

HEIGHT 5'11

HOMETOWN Luton

FAMILY Mum and Dad Jackie and David, brother called Aaron

BEFORE UNION J Jaymi was a teaching assistant, teaching singing and dancing

CELEBRITY CRUSH Rita Ora

KNOWN AS The Dad of Union J, making sure the other boys are up on time in the morning!

LIKES Animals and Twilight

RANDOM FACTS Jaymi is left-handed and can turn his feet backwards 180 degrees!

we love you...

16

GEORGE FACTFILE

NAME   George Paul Shelley

BIRTHDATE   27 July 1993

STARSIGN   Leo

HEIGHT   5'11

HOMETOWN   Clevedon

FAMILY   Mum and Dad Toni and Dominic. George has a sister, Harriet and three younger brothers, Leo, Archie and Spencer, as well as two step-sisters, Annabelle and Louisa

BEFORE UNION J   George was studying, as well as working in a local coffee shop, and card shop

CELEBRITY CRUSH   Selena Gomez and Demi Lovato

KNOWN AS   The youngest, George is the baby of the group

LIKES   Spaghetti Bolognese and bananas (not at the same time though!)

RANDOM FACTS   He has 3 hamsters and his favourite character from The Big Bang Theory is 'Sheldon'

17

we love you...

CROSSWORD

ACROSS

1   Before Union J there was? (6,1)

5   This Irish lovely was the boys' mentor on X Factor. (5,5)

6   George sang this Britney Spears hit at his first audition. (5)

7   Union J's debut single. (5,3)

11   _____ and TV Screens - what's the name of the boys' first tour? (9)

12   Harry _____ told George not to cut his hair. (6)

DOWN

2   George's middle name. (4)

3   Josh and Jaymi met at this theatre school. (6,5)

4   JJ has a phobia of these. (6,5)

8   The boys signed to this record label. (4)

9   The boys' diehard fans. (5)

10   Call me _____. They sang this song on their first performance as Union J. (5)

ANSWERS ON PAGE 60

TWEET

If you could only have one drink for the rest of your life what would it be? Hmmm..... Josh

Shorts and a Jumper. Couldn't work out if it was hot or cold! George X

CAN'T WAIT FOR TOUR!!!! WHO'S COMING!? ps... na na nana na i'm listening to single 2 right this second :P George X

You can't beat putting one arm out the car as you drive along!!!! Anyone else agree??? Josh xx

Had all my hair chopped off yesterday! I love short hair! George X

Going through all my birthday stuff sent by all u amazing people :) thankyou so so much! Your love is incredible, making me smile :D josh x

Just got back in England, re-united with boys and already feeling at home.. Jaymi and I are singing along to NSYNCs greatest hits lol! Josh

Awwww the Royal Baby is called George! We are instantly friends! Yay! #RoyalBaby nawwwwww George X

Wow this weather is insane!! Still feels like I'm on holiday. Hot hot hot. Make sure u stick sun lotion on peeps JJX

Love this show man vs food!!!! Does anyone get really hungry after watching this or just me? Lol JJX

TWOO!

@UnionJWorld
@GeorgeUnionJ
@JJUnionJ
@JaymiUnionJ
@JoshyUnionJ

RETWEET of you're coming to see us at our very own "Magazines + TV Screens" tour!!! Josh, George, JJ and Jaymi xxx

Just reading where everyone is from makes me wanna come over and have a massive hug!! Will see u all soon I'm sure :D fingers crossed! Josh

Looking at my potentch new house today, paint brushes at the ready lol , who's good at DIY? Lol cause I'm not haha Jaymi x

Hello sunshine ! Jaymi xx

My sunglasses only just fit over my huge eyebrows lol..... anyone else have that problem? Haha josh x

Just tried to get out of the car with my seatbelt on lol! Has that ever happened to you??? I feel like such an idiot haha! Josh x

had a conversation about life with a baby turtle yesterday......they are surprisingly easy to talk to lol josh x

Can't wait to go work tomoro , dunno why but I might cause sum mischief :p Jaymi x

Yey got to patt a cart horse on holiday!!! JJX

we love you...

25

20 QUESTIONS

1 What is George's favourite food?

2 What song did Triple J audition with on the X Factor?

3 Which 2 members of Union J were born in July?

4 Who dared Union J to eat pickled eggs and jellied eels for Comic Relief 2013?

5 Which member of Union J can sing in Korean?

6 Which member of Union J used to be a jockey?

7 Which member of the band tweets the most?

8 What is Josh's pet cat called?

9 Who is the youngest in the band?

10 What is the name of Union J's debut single?

11 Who is the only member of the band to be in a relationship?

12 Who has the most siblings?

13 What height is JJ?

14 How many members were there in Triple J?

15 Which musical did Josh star in when he was just 14?

16 Which American singer/songwriter have Union J said they would like to work with?

17 Which member of Union J has 17 tattoos?

18 What was the name of the band that left X Factor, allowing Union J to take their place?

19 Who was a teaching assistant before the band?

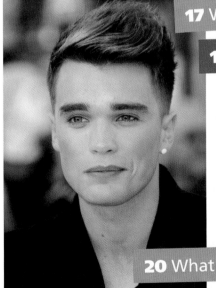

20 What facial feature is Josh well-known for?

ANSWERS ON PAGE 60

UNION J FANS

Union J may have only formed for a short while, but in that time they've gathered a strong following, and the fans like to call themselves JCats. The JCats have been a massive support to Union J - after all, they're who kept them in the X Factor for so long!

In fact even when Union J were in the live finals of the show, the JCats had formed and were speaking to each other on social network sites, to ensure their favourite four boys got through to the next stages.

And now, the JCats run loads of fan sites and pages - often getting to interact with Union J themselves on their official feeds.

The group now have now have well over a million followers on Twitter, and follow back many of the biggest JCats around.

JCats are always supportive of the boys - Jaymi got hundreds of lovely supportive messages when he came out during the X Factor live finals. They don't dislike other boy bands - instead they just concentrate on the awesomeness of Union J.

To say thanks to all the fans and to celebrate the release of their first single, Carry You, the boys drove round central London in a Union J branded black cab, then got out at Trafalgar Square and started busking to the gathered crowd!

The boys have always been grateful to their JCats, and are very much looking forward to playing to as many of them as possible during their first tour, Magazines and TV Screens, which will see Union J play dates all round the UK in December 2013 and January 2014 - we can't think of a better Christmas present!

- THE JCATS

SPOT THE DIFFERENCE

These images may look the same but they are not.

Can you spot the 8 differences between them?

ANSWERS ON PAGE 60

JJ

George

Josh

Jaymi

WHOSE SHOES?

The Union J boys are more often than not in trainers and high tops but can you match which shoes belong to JJ, George, Josh and Jaymi?

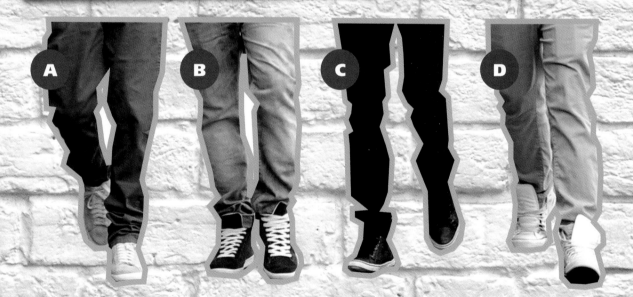

A B C D

ANSWERS ON PAGE 60

UNION J LOVE...

Singing - luckily for us!

Their families, and especially their mums - Jaymi has confessed that all four boys are mummy's boys - bless!

Cool hair - all the boys have great hair, and Harry Styles even advised George not to get his cut!

Having fun.

Animals - dogs, cats, even fish!

Twitter - over one million followers can't be wrong.

From the first auditions to rejection at bootcamp, then a lifeline just before judges' houses, Union J have come a long way since they first stepped onto the stage in front of the X Factor judges. Here's how they made it.

X FACTOR JOURNEY

We first met George as a solo artist, and he sang and played an acoustic version of the Britney Spears hit, Toxic. All the judges were impressed, and George got a yes from all three.

Triple J came on stage to screams from the audience - they had already started to make fans with the great fresh looks. When they sang a version of Rihanna's hit 'We Found Love', their fantastic harmonies and modern delivery wowed all the judges - including guest judge Rita Ora. Four yeses followed and Triple J were though to bootcamp.

At bootcamp, George was put into a 'band' with a couple of the female contestants - and they sang a version of the Labrinth hit 'Earthquakes'. Unfortunately, his performance was not to get him through and he was rejected at this stage.

Triple J fared much better at bootcamp, and had to have a sing-off with other band GMD3 for a place at the judges' houses - they sang a brilliant version of Yeah 3x by Chris Brown, but even this wasn't enough to get them to judges' houses - GMD3 took the coveted slot.

At this stage both George and Triple J were disappointed, and considering their next move.

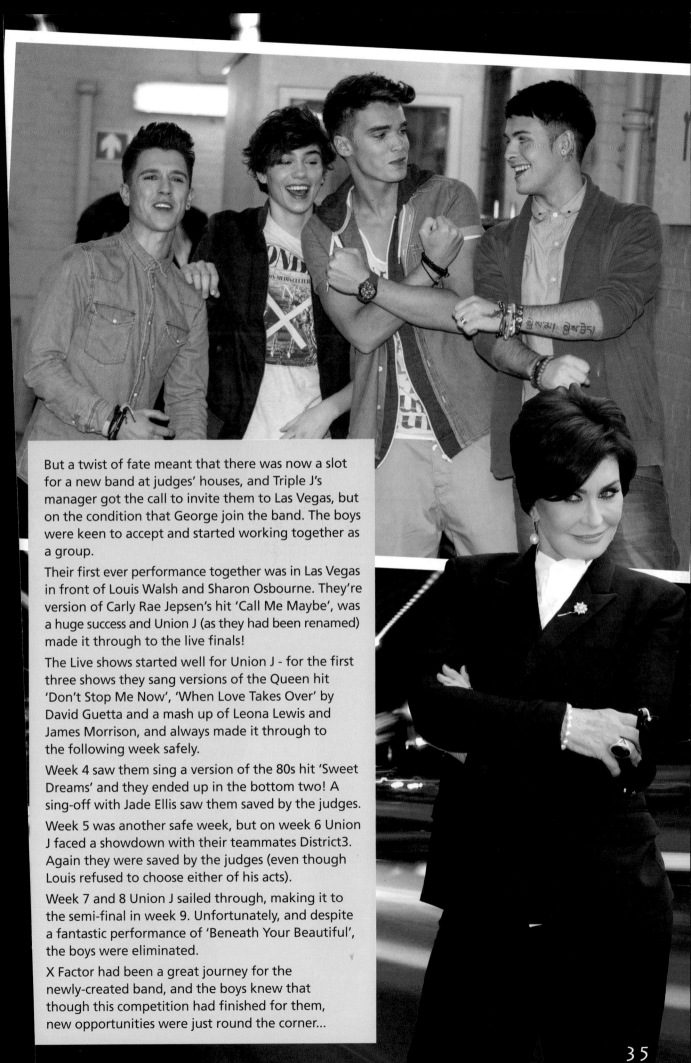

But a twist of fate meant that there was now a slot for a new band at judges' houses, and Triple J's manager got the call to invite them to Las Vegas, but on the condition that George join the band. The boys were keen to accept and started working together as a group.

Their first ever performance together was in Las Vegas in front of Louis Walsh and Sharon Osbourne. They're version of Carly Rae Jepsen's hit 'Call Me Maybe', was a huge success and Union J (as they had been renamed) made it through to the live finals!

The Live shows started well for Union J - for the first three shows they sang versions of the Queen hit 'Don't Stop Me Now', 'When Love Takes Over' by David Guetta and a mash up of Leona Lewis and James Morrison, and always made it through to the following week safely.

Week 4 saw them sing a version of the 80s hit 'Sweet Dreams' and they ended up in the bottom two! A sing-off with Jade Ellis saw them saved by the judges.

Week 5 was another safe week, but on week 6 Union J faced a showdown with their teammates District3. Again they were saved by the judges (even though Louis refused to choose either of his acts).

Week 7 and 8 Union J sailed through, making it to the semi-final in week 9. Unfortunately, and despite a fantastic performance of 'Beneath Your Beautiful', the boys were eliminated.

X Factor had been a great journey for the newly-created band, and the boys knew that though this competition had finished for them, new opportunities were just round the corner...

X FACTOR SONGS

We all loved seeing the development of the boys from solo artist (George) and band (Triple J) through the X Factor, but can you remember all the songs they sang through the auditions? If not, here's a quick recap:

GEORGE SHELLEY

★ **First Audition: Toxic,** Britney Spears

TRIPLE J

★ **First Audition: We Found Love,** Rihanna
★ **Bootcamp: Sweet Child Of Mine,** Guns and Roses
★ **Bootcamp: Yeah x 3,** Chris Brown

UNION J

★ **Judges Houses: Call Me Maybe,** Carly Rae Jepsen

LIVE SHOWS

★ **Don't Stop Me Now,** Queen

★ **Bleeding Love / Broken Strings,** Leona Lewis / James Morrison mash-up

★ **When Love Takes Over,** David Guetta

★ **Sweet Dreams,** The Eurythmics

★ **Love Story,** Taylor Swift

★ **Fix You,** Coldplay

★ **Call Me Maybe,** Carly Rae Jepsen

★ **The Winner Takes It All,** Abba

★ **I'll Be There,** Jackson 5

★ **Run,** Snow Patrol

★ **Beneath Your Beautiful,** Labrinth and Emeli Sande

★ **I'm Already There,** Lonestar

37

FASHION

The Union J boys always look great! Even in onesies!

Their style reflects their young, fun attitudes and can range from

hoodies and high tops to suits and boots. They even throw in the

occasional knitted sweater. Topshop and River

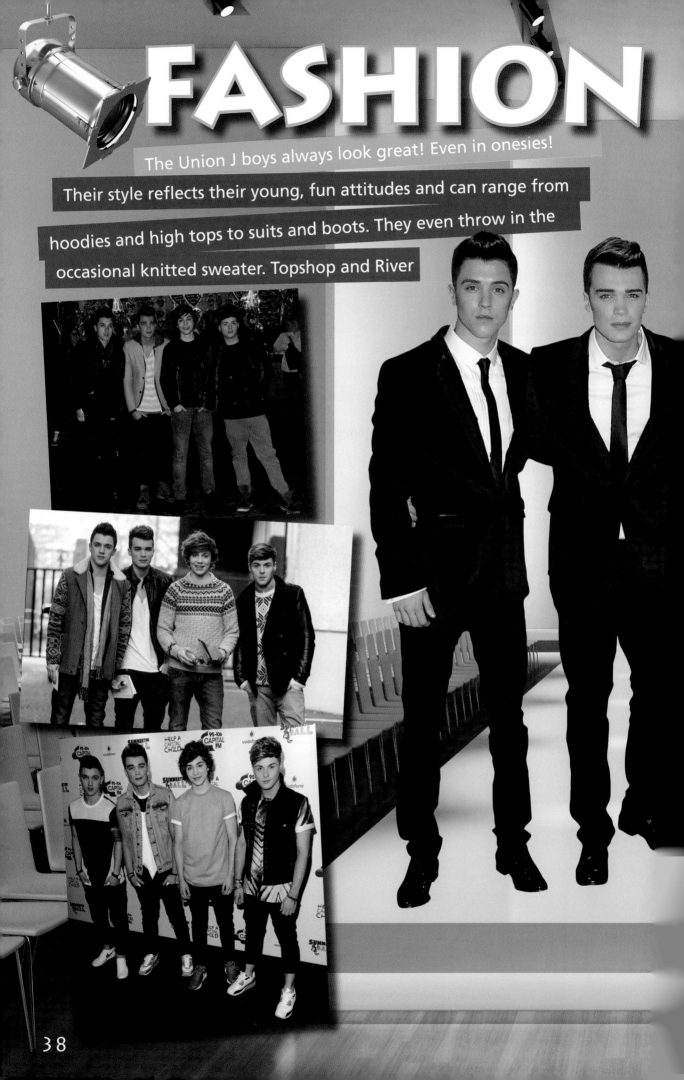

FOCUS

Island seem to be favourites, here are some

snaps of the boys working their threads.

MUSICAL INFLUENCES

JJ

Kings of Leon

Robbie Williams

The Script

Justin Bieber

George

Britney Spears

Nicki Minaj

Bruno Mars

Florence + The Machine

Ed Sheeran

The Union J boys may be a product of the X Factor, but all have a strong interest in music and take their influences from many different artists. Here are a few of their favourites:

Josh

Jessie J

Kings of Leon

Snow Patrol

Chris Brown

Michael Buble

Ne-Yo

Jaymi

Beyonce

Christina Aguilera

Whitney Houston

Cheryl

The Pussycat Dolls

41

we love you...

42

43

MISSING

Don't ever say you're ?
Just lay your ? on me
And I'll be waiting there for you
The ? can be so blinding
When you get tired of fighting
You ? the one you can look to

When the ? you have gets blurry
You don't have to worry, I'll be your ?
It's the ? I can do, cause when I ?, you pulled me through
So you know that

I'll carry you, I'll carry you, I'll carry you
So you know that
I'll carry you, I'll carry you, I'll carry you

I know it's been a ? night, but now I'm here it's alright
I don't mind walking in your shoes
We'll take each ? together, till you come back to ?
You know that I know the ? you

LYRICS

And when the ? you have gets blurry
You don't have to worry, I'll be your ?
That's the ? I can do, cause when I ? , you pulled me through
So you know that

I'll carry you, I'll carry you, I'll carry you
So you know that
I'll carry you, I'll carry you, I'll carry you

Like you've been ? for hours and can't catch your breath
The demons are ? so loud in your head
You're tired you're broken you're cut and you're ?
But nothing's too ? just hold on, I'll carry you

I'll carry you

So you know that

I'll carry you, I'll carry you, I'll carry you
So you know that
I'll carry you, I'll carry you, I'll carry you
So you know that
I'll carry you, I'll carry you, I'll carry you

ANSWERS ON PAGE 61

WORDSEARCH

Find the words in the grid. Words can go horizontally, vertically and diagonally in all eight directions.

S	N	E	E	R	C	S	V	T	H	K	M
C	R	O	T	C	A	F	X	J	H	H	N
Y	K	S	R	G	G	Q	J	A	Y	M	I
N	J	E	H	J	E	L	Y	T	G	C	M
O	G	N	R	B	G	O	K	N	A	F	M
S	U	I	N	J	Y	F	R	R	L	M	W
Q	N	Z	K	C	V	E	R	G	S	R	L
B	I	A	Y	H	B	Y	K	I	E	Z	M
N	O	G	L	S	Y	O	U	C	K	W	J
L	N	A	T	O	M	O	O	T	O	J	D
X	J	M	U	J	L	K	L	K	W	J	M
B	K	S	K	Y	S	C	R	A	P	E	R

- [ ] Book
- [ ] CarryYou
- [ ] George
- [ ] Jaymi
- [ ] JJ
- [ ] Jockey
- [ ] Josh
- [ ] Louis
- [ ] Magazines
- [ ] Skyscraper
- [ ] Sony
- [ ] TVScreens
- [ ] UnionJ
- [ ] XFactor

ANSWERS ON PAGE 61

46

EYE SPY

We've all gazed into the eyes of Union J lots I'm sure, but can you guess which pair belongs to whom?

ANSWERS ON PAGE 61

SAY WHAT?

Jaymi:
"I'm gay and I've never been happier."
The Sun

The band:
"We would absolutely like to work with Jason Derulo."
Teen Now

JJ on their single 'Carry You':
"It's a song for our fans I think; obviously they've carried us to where we are today, so it's definitely a song for them. It's very upbeat, very summery and it's just about people being there for each other and carrying each other through hard times. I hope everyone likes it as much as we do."
Scotcampus.com

JJ on One Direction and The Wanted:
"I do genuinely think we have better songs."
Top of the Pops

Josh:
"There's only so much you can do with pop."
Digitalspy.co.uk

Jaymi:
"Last night Josh made a bed out of cushions at the end of my bed and stayed at mine."
Daily Star

JJ:
"What make us different to One Direction? Um, we're a four-piece, they're a five."
Heatworld.com

Josh on George joining the band:
"It's cliché but he's the missing piece of the jigsaw puzzle."
BBC Radio 1

George on his first kiss:
"Her mum invited me over for dinner one night, and we were watching Grease. She wanted to show me her taekwondo belts because she did taekwondo and she ended up just kissing me."
sugarscape.com

George:
"I've got an undying crush on Selena Gomez. It's the Disney thing."
sugarscape.com

Josh's most cutting insult:
"You whizzer. Yeah, you whizzer."
sugarscape.com

JJ:
"Jaymi is mum. When we went to Vegas he was the one who carried the passports, so he kind of looked after us."
capitalfm.com

A-Z OF UNION J

A: Ascot - Josh is from this racing town

B: Bootcamp - all the boys got through to bootcamp stages of the X Factor auditions

C: 'Carry You' - the fantastic debut single

D: 'Don't Stop Me Now' - the boys' performance of this Queen classic at the first X Factor live finals was a hit with judges and fans

E: Eliminated - George got the boot at bootcamp, but was given a new chance as part of Union J

F: Fans - JCats!

G: Gorgeous – every one of the band

H: Hairstyles - the boys are always well-groomed!

I: Interviews - we love hearing what the boys have to say about things

J: Jockey - JJ trained as a jockey and has ridden in a race for The Queen!

K: Korean - George can sing in this Asian language

L: Love - the boys say: "we're four normal down-to-earth guys who love to sing"

M: Magazines and TV Screens – the boys' first tour

N: News - we keep up to date with the boys on Twitter

O: One Direction - they often get compared to this 'other' boy band

P: 'Pompeii' - they covered this Bastille hit for Nick Grimshaw on Radio 1

Q: Queues – there are always lots of fans waiting for the boys after their performances

R: Record Label - Union J signed to Sony in 2013

S: Single - they want debut single 'Carry You' to get to number one

T: Tattoos - Jaymi loves them and had seventeen at the last count

U: Union J of course!

V: Vine - the guys use Vine to upload news and videos

W: Walsh, Louis - their X Factor mentor

X: X Factor - where it all started

Y: 'Yeah x 3' - Triple J's version of the Chris Brown hit got them through bootcamp

Z: ZZZ - after all that work, the boys are bound to be tired!

FEED ME!

George loves the teatime classic spag bol.
Here's how to make it in a few easy steps:

- 1 onion
- 1 or 2 cloves of garlic
- 500g minced beef
- 1 1/2 tins tomatoes
- 3 carrots

- 250g button mushrooms
- mixed herbs
- Parmesan cheese
- spaghetti

Chop one large onion and cook over a low heat for about 5 mins until softened, and add garlic to taste.

Add 500g minced beef, and cook until there is no pink meat left, then add the tomatoes.

Peel and grate the carrots and add to sauce with the mushrooms and bring to the boil.

Add 1 tsp mixed herbs and simmer for about 40 mins.

Meanwhile cook spaghetti to packet instructions.

Serve up and add Parmesan to taste.

Union J also love...

Fajitas

Indian Takeaway

BBQ

Marmite

The boys also ate the following 'delicacies' for

Comic Relief 2013 (dared by Jessie J)

– Pickled Eggs, Jellied Eels

53

MUSIC TO

We love to listen to Union J, but what do the like to boys listen to?

JJ

Grenade – Bruno Mars

Sex On Fire – Kings Of Leon

Use Somebody – Kings Of Leon

As Long As You Love Me – Justin Bieber, Big Sean

Work – Iggy Azalea

Little Bird – Ed Sheeran

Nothing – The Script

If You Could See Me Now – The Script

Starships – Nicki Minaj

Firework – Katy Perry

Fix a Heart – Demi Lovato

Runaway Baby – Bruno Mars

Rabbit Heart – Florence + The Machine

Toxic – Britney Spears

You Need Me, I don't Need You – Ed Sheeran

Fantastic Baby – Big Bang

GEORGE

OUR EARS

Here are their playlists.

Who You Are – Jessie J

JOSH

Halo – Beyonce

Take You Down – Chris Brown

Forever – Chris Brown

Already Taken – Trey Songz

Sex On Fire – Kings Of Leon

Home – Michael Buble

Greatest Day – Take That

JAYMI

Love On Top – Beyonce

Run The World – Beyonce

Single Ladies – Beyonce

Fighter – Christina Aguilera

Fight For This Love – Cheryl

In My Head – Jason Derulo

Hush Hush; Hush Hush – The Pussycat Dolls

Run To You – Whitney Houston

THE FUTURE

As the next series of the X Factor enters its final stages, Jaymi, JJ, Josh and George must be sitting back wondering what has happened to them in the last 12 months - from bootcamp rejects to finalists, to successful artists in their own right.

Last year has certainly been a crazy one for Union J, but next year will be just as busy! Now that the boys have completely merged as a group and know what they want to achieve, there's going to be a lot of hard work to fit in, but a lot of fun too!

FOR UNION J

One of the biggest things happening next year is Union J's first solo tour (they of course were on tour with the rest of the X Factor finalists at the start of 2013). The UK wide tour runs in December 2013 and January 2014, heading to venues all over the country, from Plymouth to Glasgow. We've got our tickets already, and are very much looking forward to hearing the boys sing live - their harmonies were always amazing on the X Factor, and we're sure they've been practising loads to ensure their performance on tour is spot on.

If that wasn't enough, the Union J debut album is released at the end of the year - as yet untitled; it will include the hit first single 'Carry You', and many more of our favourite hits to come.

Exploring their musical influences has always been important to the boys, and next year might see them collaborate with some of the people they admire most. In the past Union J have said that they'd love to work with Jason Derulo, and after an appearance on a Radio show, Jason said he really liked the single 'Carry You', and that he'd also like to work with them, saying that he'd make it happen. We can't wait for such collaboration, and are sure it will be a great one.

They boys spent a week filling in as celebrity reporters on ITV's Daybreak in the summer of 2013, and seemed to really enjoy themselves - maybe we'll be seeing more of them in front of the camera next year?

We're just looking forward to hearing more songs from Union J next year - we've seen them loads in interviews, and following them on Twitter means we can hear what they're up to almost every day, but we fell in love with the boys watching them perform every week on X Factor and hearing their great voices, and that's what we want more of in 2014 - hope you're taking note boys!

Union J

MAGAZINES + TV SCREENS *Tour*

DECEMBER

14 OXFORD NEW THEATRE
15 CARDIFF MOTORPOINT ARENA
16 SHEFFIELD CITY HALL
18 PLYMOUTH PAVILIONS
19 BRIGHTON CENTRE
21 MANCHESTER O2 APOLLO
22 BOURNEMOUTH INT. CENTRE
23 LONDON HAMMERSMITH APOLLO (MATINEE SHOW)
23 LONDON HAMMERSMITH APOLLO

28 NEWCASTLE CITY HALL
29 NOTTINGHAM ROYAL CONCERT HALL

JANUARY

03 IPSWICH REGENT
05 BRISTOL COLSTON HALL
06 LIVERPOOL ARENA
07 GLASGOW CLYDE AUDITORIUM
09 BLACKPOOL OPERA HOUSE
10 BIRMINGHAM NIA

BUY ONLINE AT
TICKETMASTER.CO.UK | LIVENATION.CO.UK
W W W . U N I O N J O F F I C I A L . C O M
A LIVE NATION PRESENTATION IN ASSOCIATION WITH CAA & CROWN TALENT & MEDIA GROUP

QUIZ ANSWERS

CROSSWORD p21

```
        T R I P L E J   S
        A           Y
      L O U I S W A L S H
R       L           V I
U       T O X I C   C
B                   A Y
B                   O
E   C A R R Y Y O U N
R       Y   J       U
B   S O N Y   C   M M A B E
A       S   C A T S   A G   S
N       T Y L E S       Z I N E S
D   S T Y L E S         B
```

WHOSE SHOES? p31

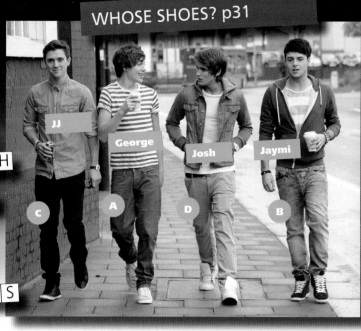

JJ George Josh Jaymi

C   A   D   B

QUIZ p26-27

1 Spaghetti Bolognese

2 'We Found Love' by Rihanna

3 George and Josh

4 Jessie J   **5** George

6 JJ   **7** JJ   **8** Oreo

9 George   **10** Carry You   **11** Jaymi, with boyfriend Olly

12 George   **13** 5'10   **14** 3   **15** Chitty Chitty Bang Bang

16 Jason Derulo   **17** Jaymi   **18** Rough Copy

19 Jaymi   **20** His well-styled eyebrows!

SPOT THE DIFFERENCE p30

BIOSONG

CARRY YOU

Don't ever say you're **lonely**
Just lay your **problems** on me
And I'll be waiting there for you
The **stars** can be so blinding
When you get tired of fighting
You **know** the one you can look to

When the **vision** you have gets blurry
You don't have to worry, I'll be your **eyes**
It's the **least** I can do, cause when I **fell**, you
pulled me through
So you know that

I'll carry you, I'll carry you, I'll carry you
So you know that
I'll carry you, I'll carry you, I'll carry you

I know it's been a **long** night, but now I'm
here it's alright
I don't mind walking in your shoes
We'll take each **step** together, till you come
back to **center**
You know that I know the **real** you

When the **vision** you have gets blurry
You don't have to worry, I'll be your **eyes**
It's the **least** I can do, cause when I **fell**, you
pulled me through
So you know that

I'll carry you, I'll carry you, I'll carry you
So you know that
I'll carry you, I'll carry you, I'll carry you

Like you've been **running** for hours and
can't catch your breath
The demons are **screaming** so loud in your
head
You're tired you're broken you're cut and
you're **bruised**
But nothing's too **heavy** just hold on, I'll
carry you

I'll carry you

So you know that

I'll carry you, I'll carry you, I'll carry you
So you know that
I'll carry you, I'll carry you, I'll carry you
So you know that
I'll carry you, I'll carry you, I'll carry you

S	N	E	E	R	C	S	V	T	H	K	M
C	R	O	T	C	A	F	X	J	H	K	N
Y	K	S	R	G	G	Q	J	A	Y	M	I
N	J	E	H	J	E	L	Y	T	G	C	M
O	G	N	R	B	G	O	K	N	A	F	M
S	U	I	N	J	Y	F	R	R	L	M	W
Q	N	Z	K	C	V	E	R	G	S	R	L
B	I	A	Y	H	B	Y	K	I	E	Z	M
N	O	G	L	S	Y	O	U	C	K	W	J
L	N	A	T	O	M	O	O	T	O	J	D
X	J	M	U	J	L	K	L	K	W	J	M
B	K	S	K	Y	S	C	R	A	P	E	R

JJ

Josh

George

Jaymi

WHERE'S UNION J?